Length of Holes on the Old Course.

Hole Nº	Name	Yards	Hole Nº	Name	Yards
1	Burn	370	10	Bobby Jones	318
2	Dyke	411	11	High coming home	172
3	Cartgate going out	352	12	Heathery coming home	316
4	Ginger Beer	419	13	Hole o'Cross coming home	398
5	Hole o'Cross going out	514	14	Long	523
6	Heathery going out	374	15	Cartgate coming home	401
7	High going out	359	16	Corner of the Dyke	351
8	Short	178	17	Road	461
9	End	307	18	Tom Morris	354

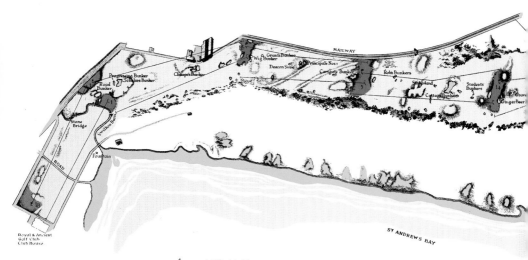

Surveyed & Depicted by

A. Mackenzie

Golf Course Architect
March 1924

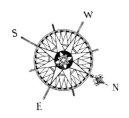

The
OLD COURSE, ST. ANDREWS

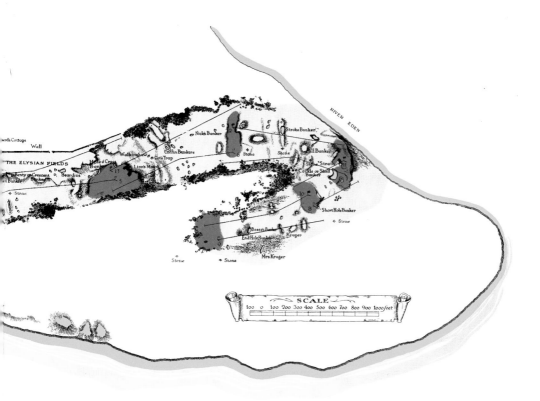

RIVER EDEN

Edwards Cottage

Wall

THE ELYSIAN FIELDS

Plenty Crescent
Bunker Bunkers

Stone

Walkinshaw

Hole o'Cross
Bunker

Lion's Mouth

Beardies

Nick's Bunker

Coffin Bunkers

Cat's Trap

13

5

Stroke Bunker

Stone

Hill Bunker

Strath

Cockle or Shell
Bunker

Stone

6

8

Short Hole Bunker

Stone

Boase's Bunker

Kruger

End Hole Bunker

Mrs Kruger

Stone

Stone

SCALE
100 0 100 200 300 400 500 600 700 800 900 1000 feet

The Spirit
of
St. Andrews

The Spirit
of
St. Andrews

BY
Alister MacKenzie

FOREWORD BY
Robert Tyre Jones, Jr.

Broadway Books

NEW YORK

BROADWAY

Broadway Books titles may be purchased for business or promotional use or for special sales. For information, please write to: Special Markets Department, Bantam Doubleday Dell Publishing Group, Inc., 1540 Broadway, New York, NY 10036.

BROADWAY BOOKS and its logo, a letter B bisected on the diagonal, are trademarks of Broadway Books, a division of Bantam Doubleday Dell Publishing Group, Inc.

First Broadway Books trade paperback edition published 1998.

Library of Congress Cataloging-in-Publication Data

Mackenzie, A. (Alexander), b. 1870.
The spirit of St. Andrews / by Alister Mackenzie : foreword by Robert Tyra Jones, Jr.—1st Broadway Books trade pbk. ed.
p. cm.
Originally published: Chelsea, Mich. : Sleeping Bear Press, c1995.
ISBN 0-7679-0169-X (pbk.)
1. Golf. 2. Golf courses. 3. Golf courses—Maintenance and repair. 4. Royal and Ancient Golf Club of St. Andrews—History.
I. Title. [GV965.M178 1998]
796.352—dc21 97-37063 CIP

98 99 00 01 02 10 9 8 7 6 5 4 3 2 1

✻ *Contents* ✻

�֍ *Acknowledgements* ✦

The Spirit of St. Andrews is a book that was destined to be published. For all the times that the manuscript could have
been accidently thrown away or lost over the 60 years since
it was written—it simply defied the odds.

We have published the book as it would have been in
1934. We used photos whenever possible from that era. The
book that you have is almost precisely as MacKenzie wrote it,
as we did not want to alter his unique and wonderfully entertaining style.

Many thanks to Jim Langley, Barry Staley, Ben Crenshaw,
James Scott, Ron Whitten, Robert Laubach, Steven Hammon,
Mike DeVries, Peter Richardson, Sid Matthew, Tom Doak, the
USGA, the Royal & Ancient, and so many others who have
helped both Ray Haddock and the publisher bring this book
to fruition—we acknowledge their efforts and dedication.

❧ *Foreword* ❧

An astonishing amount of golf—that is, good golf—is played between the ears. We have to think, to concentrate on the stroke, in order to hit the ball correctly. If this were not so I doubt if we should trouble ourselves to play the game.

In the same way, we want our golf courses to make us think. However much we may enjoy whaling the life out of the little white ball, we soon grow tired of playing a golf course that does not give us problems in strategy as well as skill.

Dr. Alister MacKenzie is unquestionably one of the world's foremost designers of golf courses. Examples of his work are among the best known courses of this country and the British Isles. It is paying his work the highest possible compliment to say that all his courses that I have played have been interesting; in every instance he has placed interest and enjoyment ahead of difficulty.

In large measure, the popularity which the game of golf will enjoy in the future depends on the quality of the courses we provide for the players of the future. A great majority of the players, then as now, will be "average golfers." Our courses must be built for them as well as for the "scratch man."

Dr. MacKenzie has proved that it is entirely possible to construct a course that will provide interesting yet not unreasonable problems for every golfer according to his skill.

Every golfer worthy of the name should have some acquaintance with the principles of golf course design, not only for the betterment of the game, but for his own selfish enjoyment. Let him know a good hole from a bad one and the reasons for a bunker here and another there, and he will be a long way towards pulling his score down to respectable limits. When he has taught himself to study a hole from the point of view of the man who laid it out, he will be much more likely to play it correctly.

Like myself, Dr. MacKenzie is a lover of old St. Andrews. Of course, like everyone else, he despairs of ever producing anything quite so good, but the doctor's experience with camouflage and his innate artistry enable him to convert an inland terrain into something surprisingly like the seaside links land, which is the very best golfing country.

In this book, written by a man who has made almost a life study of the subject, will be found much of interest to any golfer. It presents a chance for the golf enthusiast to extend his education to a very important and very absorbing phase of the game.

Robt. T. Jones, Jr.

Robt. T. Jones, Jr.

⚜ *Introduction* ⚜

"I have always wanted to live where one could practice shots in one's pyjamas before breakfast, and at Santa Cruz the climate is so delightful that one can play golf every day of the year."
—Dr. A. MacKenzie

It is nearing Christmas 1932 and the place is the cottage that Dr. MacKenzie has built for his wife Hilda on the 6th fairway at Pasatiempo Golf Course. Joining them for the holidays are her son Tony, with his wife and their two sons Philip and Raymund, who have just recently arrived from England. Little more than one year later, on January 6, 1934, the Doctor dies and his ashes are distributed over the golf course.

Alexander MacKenzie was born in England on August 30, 1870 in the town of Normanton, County of York. He was a well-educated man, receiving several degrees from Cambridge and from Leeds, where he practiced medicine before going to South Africa to serve as a civil surgeon in the Boer War. Here he could not help but admire the capacity of the Boers to conceal themselves so effectively. It was these observations that first interested him in "the imitation of nature," and which led to his appointment to establish the British School of Camouflage during World War I.

Although he had played golf in his youth, he did not take up the game seriously until after he received his degrees, when he "developed the disease badly." Yet he did not become a good golfer until into his 60's. He was known as Dr. Alister MacKenzie during his golf course design career, which had begun shortly after his return from the Boer War. "I was a keen golfer, and while studying camouflaged defenses it struck me that inland golf courses could be vastly improved, not only from the point of view of beauty, but in creating interesting strategic problems by the imitation of the natural features characteristic of the only golf courses which were at that time worthwhile, namely, the sand dunes by the sea. I then became one of the pioneers of modern golf course architecture and wrote the first book on the subject."

His first course was Alwoodley in Yorkshire, followed by Moortown, Sandmoor, Sitwell Park, the Eden Course at St. Andrews (with H.S. Colt) and many others. It was his two-shot hole design in a contest sponsored by Charles Blair Macdonald in the magazine *Country Life,* which was awarded first prize by judges Horace Hutchinson and Bernard Darwin, that jumped him into national prominence in 1914. This design, somewhat altered, was used as the basis for the 18th hole at the Lido Golf Club in New York.

In 1926, he made his famous "world tour," his reputation having preceded him around the world. He took the long way, through the Suez Canal, making several stops in and along Australia and New Zealand, from which arose such magnificent courses as Royal Melbourne, Royal Queensland and Titirangi. He also designed the two courses at the Jockey Club in Buenos Aires and Mar De Plata in Argentina. In 1927, before he returned to California to design the Cypress Point Club on the Monterey Peninsula, he was called to remodel Lahinch and other courses in Ireland. Several of his courses still remain among the "Top 100," including Cypress Point, Pasatiempo at Santa Cruz, Crystal Downs in upper Michigan, and the home of the Masters, Augusta National. Many more of his courses were completed after his death, including the University of Michigan and the Gray and Scarlet courses at Ohio State University.

The Spirit of St. Andrews is MacKenzie's second book, and was written and compiled in 1933 with the help of his stepson, my father Tony Haddock. It was not published then, but has lain forgotten like many family treasures until recently brought to light among my father's papers.

The Spirit of St. Andrews leads the reader through the evolution of golf at St. Andrews to modern day golf course design, through the secrets of the golf swing that made him the most improved golfer at Pasatiempo, to an analysis of what constitutes an ideal hole, and even his economic philosophy. With stories by and about Bobby Jones, Walter Hagen and many others of his time, we are given an intimate look into his delightful and original personality. He was a great fellow and a great architect. He did a lot for golf, and this book is dedicated to golfers everywhere in his memory.

—Raymund M. Haddock

DR. A. MACKENZIE

❖1❖
The Evolution of Golf

G olf, in its early days, was always played on commons or links land which bordered the sea. The natural characteristics of this type of land made it easily the most suitable for the game. It is an interesting fact that sandy gravelly soil which is of little value for agricultural purposes is by far the best type of land for a golf course. Links land, consisting as it does of rolling sand dune country partially covered with gorse, heather, bent and short "rabbity" turf, is specially suitable.

In days of old, a golf course was usually kept by one greenkeeper who not infrequently acted as professional as well. Rabbits acted as the "grounds staff," keeping the turf short, crisp and free from weeds. The duties of the greenkeeper merely consisted in cutting holes and sweeping rabbit droppings from the greens. Now, alas, most of these old seaside courses have been ruined by well-intentioned but injudicious efforts of their green committees to improve on nature. The rabbits have been killed off. Alkaline fertilizers, fit only for agriculture, have been used, with the result that the sparse dwarf velvety turf has disappeared and is now replaced by plantains, daisies, clover, and luscious agricultural grasses, which need an enormous amount of mowing, weeding and upkeep.

Michael Hurdzan

Old Tom Morris—thoroughly steeped in the traditions and spirit of the game

The more money these clubs have had to spend, the more their courses have deteriorated. Not only has the turf been ruined, but there has been a wanton destruction of many of the natural features. The greens have been flattened out, sand hazards which created the interest and strategy of the holes have been filled up, and in too many cases even the undulations of the fairways have been destroyed. The features of the links land, which the modern golf course architect attempts to imitate, sometimes with indifferent success, have disappeared, so that these glorious natural courses have only too frequently become as dull and insipid as a second rate inland course.

There was a course in the wilds of the west coast of Scotland among most spectacular sand dunes named Machrihanish. It was scores of miles from any railway station and the only way to get to it was by steamboat and a long carriage drive. Notwithstanding its inaccessibility, the course was so good, and the climate so bracing, that it became very popular and attracted an increasing number of men who had reputations as players. Some of these players were open or amateur champions, and the natives, dazzled by their reputations, avidly agreed to their suggestions for "improving the course." I have been visiting Machrihanish at intervals for over thirty years and each time I have found that the course has appreciably deteriorated.

When I made my first visit, the course was kept by one greenkeeper, it was not mown except by the rabbits, nor was it rolled. The greenkeeper's duties consisted in simply cutting the holes and filling up any scrapes the rabbits might have made on the fairways and greens. This was rarely necessary, as rabbits very seldom scrape well-trodden turf, but confine their attentions to bare places on the outskirts of the course. Even the depredations of the rabbits therefore involved remarkably little labour, and in these early days the turf on the greens and fairways was superior to any I have seen before or since. There was a complete freedom from weeds, daisies, or worm casts, and one's ball sat up on the closely cropped turf in a remarkable manner. Each hole was an adventure. There were no guiding flags and no fixed routes. One could frequently beat an opponent who had greater length and skill by superior strategy.

The course was planned by Old Tom Morris. The annual subscription was ten shillings and there was no initiation fee. Old Tom was thoroughly steeped in the traditions and spirit of the game. He was a sportsman in the best sense of the word and he had no use for arguments based on strict equity. No professional since his time has ever grasped the real sporting spirit of golf architecture like he did.

The founder of Machrihanish was another remarkable man. His name was Stuart and he held the rank of Commander in the Navy. The story ran that he had been kicked out of the service for knocking down an Admiral.

❧ Stuart was called on to give evidence in the case of the Haskell ball patent, and proved that he and Old Tom Morris manufactured a rubber covered ball long before the "Haskell" had been invented. He told me that he had conceived the idea from seeing strings of elastic protruding from ladies' elastic sided boots. He thought that if similar elastic strands were strung tightly round a central core and covered with gutta percha, a ball of great resiliency could be made. During his evidence, so he told me, the judge asked him, "Can you tell me, Commander Stuart, of any man except you and Tom Morris who played with your rubber cored ball in those days?" "Yes," he replied, "your own father, sir." This clinched the case against the Haskell people. ☙

Commander Stuart told me that when he and Old Tom first saw Machrihanish they stood on "yonder hillock" and Old Tom looked round in a spirit of deep reverence and said, "Eh Mon! The Almichty had Gowf in his e'e when he made this place!"

As the years go by, Machrihanish is steadily deteriorating. The rabbits have been destroyed on the clubhouse side of the burn, and as a consequence the beautiful velvety turf has been replaced by rich agricultural grasses, daisies, and weeds, whilst on the other side of the burn where there are millions of rabbits, the old character of the turf still remains. As the club accumulates more funds, however, they are used to destroy the gorgeous natural features.

Some of the natural greens were so undulating that at times one had to putt twenty or thirty yards round to lay dead at a hole only five yards away. These greens have all gone and today one loses all the joy of outwitting an opponent by making spectacular putts of this description.

In an effort to eliminate "unfairness," many of the natural hazards have been destroyed, undulations shaved off, and alternative routes to holes done away with, and the interest and strategy of the course has disappeared. The ultimate result of all this has been to make the course infinitely more unfair and has, moreover, destroyed the skill, interest and pleasurable excitement of the game. It is sorrowful history that the same tale can be told of so many of the British seaside courses.

Almost without exception the old seaside rabbity turf has disappeared, being replaced by grasses entirely unsuitable for golf. The turf near the clubhouse is usually worse than that further away, as on many of the seaside links there still remain a few rabbits on the outskirts of the course.

⋈ St. Andrews ⋈

Fortunately there is one which has been described as a much abused old course in the little kingdom of Fife, Scotland, which has so far escaped destruction by vandals in the shape of amateur golf architects. I refer to Old St. Andrews. This is partially owing to the fact that the members have considered it too sacred to be touched, and it is also due to the opposition of such stalwarts as the late John L. Low, the

Blackwells, the Hambros, Norman Boase, and many others to suggested changes.

St. Andrews still retains its pristine charm. I doubt if even in a hundred years' time a course will be made which has such interesting strategic problems and which creates such enduring and increasing pleasurable excitement and varied shots. No one knows who was the designer of the course. Like Topsy in *Uncle Tom's Cabin,* it "simply growed."

It is obvious that no one knew anything about golf course architecture in the early days of St. Andrews. It may even have been planned by someone who had never seen a golf course. Someone, perhaps, who had heard of the game and went cutting holes three or four hundred yards apart on attractive plateaus, where long white feathers stuck in the holes would be visible, until he got to the end of the available playing area. This much, however, is certain: previous to 1859 the inward nine holes, with the exception of the 18th, were originally played back to the holes doing duty for the outward nine.

As more golfers began to play at St. Andrews, this gave rise to congestion, and fresh holes were cut for the inward nine. Formerly the course was very narrow and bordered by whin bushes, but these bushes gradually disappeared and the links became wider and wider. This additional width enabled the outward and the inward holes to be played as they are today. Nevertheless, with the exception of the 1st, 9th, 17th and 18th holes, both the outgoing and ingoing holes are played on the same greens.

One could talk for weeks about the Old Course at St. Andrews. Those who belong to the penal school of golf are only too ready to condemn it and suggest that its reputation is solely due to tradition.

My experience is exactly the opposite. I am by nature a revolutionary, and only too apt to scoff at tradition. Before visiting St. Andrews I had what were considered revolutionary ideas regarding golf courses. To my astonishment, when I inspected the Old Course I found my ideals in actual practice. I have been a staunch supporter of the Old Course ever

6

since, and have always opposed suggested alterations to it. Some time later I was employed by the club to make a plan of the Old Course, which is reproduced inside the front cover of this book.

It took me a full year to complete the task, notwithstanding the fact that I thought I knew the course thoroughly. In actual fact I found that my knowledge was of the slightest, and the subtleties which I discovered have always been a source of amazement to me. After I had made the plan and it had appeared in its printed form, I discovered several mistakes and omissions which have, so far, fortunately been overlooked by anyone else.

Some years ago, my friend Bertie Taylor, who was nearly sixty years of age, playing against most of the leading British golfers, won the medals at the Spring and Autumn meetings at St. Andrews. At the dinner after the September medal, he was kind enough to attribute his victories to the close study he had made of this plan. He stated that he had played St. Andrews scores of times every year for twenty years but he never really knew it until he had studied the plan I had made.

Another criticism of the course, however, was obtained from my old friend Joshua Crane, a very able man and an exceptionally fine golfer who had the temerity, after playing it on three occasions, to rank it the worst of all British Championship courses. Shortly afterwards I noticed he took a house for two months at St. Andrews and played the Old Course daily, which at any rate was an indication that he was inconsistent enough to enjoy playing it.

Joshua Crane wrote many articles in American and British papers on the rating of golf courses. I do not remember all of his system, but I think he gave so many marks for the presence of rough, so many more for adequate punishment of topped shots, so many for the absence of undulating fairways and so on. Max Behr (a finalist in the 1908 U.S. Amateur Championship) and I spent a very pleasant fortnight with him at St. Andrews. It was really most unfair because we were two to one but we chaffed him unmercifully. This is the kind of conversation that occurred:

7

Tom Doak

The 2nd green at St. Andrews, with its characteristic undulations. MacKenzie was the consulting architect for the Old Course.

❧ "Tell us, Joshua, how it is you took a house at St. Andrews after rating it the worst of all championship courses. You admit you love St. Andrews." Joshua, replying in a tone which suggests that his system of rating is similar to the Laws of the Medes and Persians: "Well, it comes out last in my rating."

"Then that simply proves that your rating is wrong, and we suggest to you that if you turn your list of 'order of merit' upside down you will be right. Let us analyze your system. You give so many marks for rough; we suggest that this be reversed and that it should read 'absence of rough.' Golfers play for pleasure and surely they should not be subjected to the annoyance and irritation of searching for lost balls. It is no fun looking for your own ball and even less searching for your opponent's." Joshua, somewhat haughtily: "But do you suggest that a hole should be played with a putter?"

"That is precisely what we do suggest. No hole can be considered perfect unless it can be played with a putter." Joshua, a bit puzzled: "Why?"

"Everyone should be allowed to enjoy a golf game, including even old gentlemen of ninety, and children of five or six. Some of them cannot drive further than a good player armed with a putter. Moreover, a stretch of rough extending a hundred yards from the tee is of no earthly interest to a scratch man but may be intensely irritating to a beginner." Joshua: "Do you then consider it fair that two men should drive perfect balls and one of them should have to play from a hanging lie and the other from a level stance?"

"We do. We consider it absolutely fair and we believe that one of the great charms of the British championship courses that you admire so much is these undulating fairways. They simply differentiate between a first class player like yourself, who is able to play from a hanging lie, and others, like ourselves, who are not so skillful. Apparent luck of this kind is always, in the long run, to the advantage of the first class player." ❧

Joshua took all this chaff with the greatest possible good nature and we were all the better friends at the end of the fortnight than we were at the beginning. We honestly believe, especially after this fortnight's discussion with him, that his rating of the merit of the golf courses was entirely wrong, and should be reversed.

If he was right, then those courses constructed in the "dark ages" of golf thirty years ago—courses designed with a complete absence of variety, with a straight line of rough in front of the tee, and two straight lines bordering the fairway, with a cross bunker for the drive, and another for the second shot—would have been perfect.

Some of the old stalwarts at St. Andrews, not knowing what a good fellow he was, resented Joshua Crane's criticisms and were inclined to take him too seriously. They loved St. Andrews, but did not know why they loved it. They knew Joshua was wrong, but did not know why he was wrong. After all, the worth of a golf course cannot be judged on mathematical lines; the crucial test is what gives the most lasting and increasing pleasure.

❧ A Golf Crazy Community ❧

At St. Andrews there are two other excellent courses—the New and the Eden (designed by MacKenzie & H. S. Colt)—which, if they were not overshadowed by the Old Course, would probably be considered the best in Britain. On the Old Course there is a continuous stream of players—men, women and children—playing all the year from daylight to dark. At St. Andrews I have seen women wheeling their babies in perambulators and playing round the Jubilee Course—the course where you play for two pence a round.

The whole community is just golf crazy. During the 1930 Amateur Championship three perfect strangers shouted across the road to me, "Bobby Jones is three up!" Their appreciation of a good golfer is so great that they would have been bitterly disappointed if a Britisher had won.

Even the caddies at St. Andrews are quite different to anywhere else. Their knowledge and advice on the course makes them look on themselves as the principal partners in the match. In describing a match they use the personal pronoun "I," not even "We," and say, "I skelped an iron on to the first green," and so on.

A good caddie is undoubtedly an enormous asset at St. Andrews. I remember in the last Walker Cup match there, seeing Bobby Jones and Watts Gunn playing the fourteenth hole. They were not going too well and Bobby hit a long but slightly sliced tee shot. Watts Gunn wished to play direct for the hole, but his caddie insisted, quite rightly, that he should play at right angles to the left. Watts Gunn, after consultation with Bobby, finally did as he was told, and this was the turning point of the match and enabled the Americans to beat the British by one point.

Not only the caddies but the professionals and starters are absolute autocrats at St. Andrews.

❧ Some years ago there was a starter named Greig. He was a magnificent man with the autocratic face of the Kaiser, but better looking. When anyone crossed the road on the first fairway, you could hear his voice shouting "FORRRRRE," reverberating holes away. I was once on the first tee waiting to play, and there was a lady with a large picture hat walking haughtily down the road. Greig put his head out of his box and in a voice like thunder bellowed "F O R R R E." She took no notice. Again he bellowed forth his "F O R R R E," and, she still taking no notice, I said, "Shall I have a shot at her Greig?" "Na, na," he replied, "yer micht miss herrr, but yer could na miss her ha-a-at." ❧

❧ At one time I had the reputation of being the slowest player in Europe. At that time we played four ball matches three times a day, our first round starting at 8:30 in the morning. Greig did not like to attack me about my slowness, as I had got several jobs for his relatives as greenkeepers, but he began one day to harangue a four ball match in front of us. "Hurry up a bit there," he said. "None o' yer fiddlin' aboot playin' yer putts ower agen on the greens. Some o' us want to go to bed the nicht." This was at 8:30 in the morning. I then teed up and was taking my usual number of waggles when Greig looked up at me solemnly and said, "And the same remarks apply to you." ✖

Andrew Kirkaldy, the club professional, is another well beloved character. He wrote a book which is entitled, I believe, *Fifty Years of Golf*. One day when he was going up to London to see his publishers, he was advised to see a specialist at the same time about his lumbago. The specialist examined him and then said, "Mr. Kirkaldy, I would advise you to give up whiskey." Andrew immediately seized his hat and made for the door. "Mr. Kirkaldy," the specialist called out to him, "you have forgotten to pay me three guineas for my advice." Andrew turned and looked at him. "I'm na takkin' yer advice," he said, and turned and walked out.

When I was making the plan of the Old Course I was anxious to find the names of the old bunkers. Now there is a small bunker adjoining "Hell" bunker and I could find no one who could tell me its name until I asked one of the oldest caddies. "It is called The Pulpit," he said. "Why is it called the Pulpit?" I asked him, and the answer came back pat: "Because you can see Hell out of it."

The Scots take three things very seriously. Their golf, their religion, and their politics.

A friend of mine once told me that he was on a yacht in the Western Highlands. His host said to them "We must all go to church tomorrow." There was a general chorus of protest: Why should they go to church? Couldn't they play golf instead? Their host answered, "If we do not go to church the natives will look on us as absolute heathen and we won't be able to get any butter or milk or chickens, so, go we must."

Next day, when the minister saw these fifty or sixty English come into his kirk he preached a sermon against the wickedness of the English and finished up by saying, "an' so ma freens, ye will all go to Hell, and when you are in Hell you will cry to the Lord and say 'Oh Lord, we never kent it was a place like this, and the Lord in His infinite mercy and kindness will say (thumping the pulpit) 'Well you ken it noo."

Their political outlook is illustrated with another story of a kirk and concerns a minister, a keen politician, who, during the big split in the Liberal party, remarked from the pulpit, "Oh Lord may the great Leeberal party hang together ———." "Hear-r-r, hear-r-r," came from a staunch Conservative at the back of the kirk.

The minister was not disturbed by the interruption, but continued, "before I was interrupted by that deeseecrator of the Lor-rd's Hoose, I was aboot to say 'May the great Leeberal party hang together in accor-rd and concor-rd." The voice came again from the back of the kirk, "I'm no carin' what sort of cor-rd it is they hang by provided it is a strong cor-rd."

I shall have more to say about the Old Course at St. Andrews in subsequent chapters, but for the moment it is sufficient to say that I do not know of a single example of a successful golf course architect who is not enamoured of the Old Course and the strategic principals embodied in it.

⚔ Some Qualifications of a Golf Architect ⚔

The advent of the golf architect has done much to increase the sporting and dramatic element in golf. The true test of the value of his work is its popularity, and judging by the rapid increase in members, even on the mere rumor that the services of a well-known course architect are to be obtained, there can be no doubt the modern constructor of courses has achieved this. I know examples of the reconstruction of one or two short holes bringing in over one hundred fresh members to a club which had been steadily losing members for years.

There are many and varied qualities required for the making of a successful golf architect.

In the first place, he must have an intimate knowledge of the theory of playing the game, although it is not essential that he himself should be a good player. He may have some physical disability which prevents his becoming so, but as the training of the golf architect is purely mental and not physical, this should not prevent him from being a successful designer of courses. In any case the possession of a vivid imagination, which is an absolute essential in obtaining success, may prevent him attaining a position among the higher ranks of players. Everyone knows how fatal the imagination is in playing the game. Let the fear of socketing (shanking) once enter your head and you promptly socket every shot afterwards.

His knowledge of the game should be so intimate that he knows instinctively what is likely to produce good golf and good golfers. He must have more than a passing acquaintance with the best courses and the best golfing holes. It is not only necessary that he should play them but he should also study them and analyze the features which make them what they are. He must have a sense of proportion and be able to differentiate between essentials and nonessentials. He should be able to distinguish between those features which are of supreme importance in the making of a hole and those which are of less value.

He must have judgement in the choice of features which can be readily and cheaply reproduced, and avoid those which are impossible to construct without an inordinate expenditure of labour. How frequently has one seen large sums of money wasted in a futile attempt to reproduce the Alps, the Himalayas, or the Cardinal. Features of this kind look absolutely out of place unless the surrounding ranges of hills which harmonize with them can also be reproduced. To do this would involve the expenditure of literally millions of dollars. How often are attempts made to copy a hole, and the subtle slopes and undulations which are the making of the original overlooked.

The golf course architect must have the "sporting instinct," and if he has had a training in many and varied branches of sport and has analyzed those characteristics which provide a maximum of pleasurable excitement in them, so much the better. It is essential that he should eliminate his own game entirely, and look upon all constructional work in a purely impersonal manner. He should be able to put himself in the position of the best player that ever lived, and at the same time be extremely sympathetic towards the beginner and long handicap player.

He should, above all, have a sense of proportion and be able to come to a prompt decision as to what is the greatest good for the greatest number.

He should not be unduly influenced by hostile criticism, but should give most sympathetic consideration to criticism of a constructive nature. Not infrequently a long handicap man makes a brilliant suggestion which can often be utilized in a modified form. A knowledge of psychology gained in my medical training has been of great service in estimating what is likely to give the greatest pleasure to the greatest number.

It by no means follows that what appears to be attractive at first sight will be so permanently. A good golf course grows on one like a good painting, good music, or any other artistic creation.

A good golf course architect should have made a study, from a golfing point of view, of agricultural chemistry, botany and geology. He should also have some knowledge of map-reading, surveying and interpretation of aerial photographs. There are all sorts of details visible in an aerial photograph which are often overlooked after the most careful survey in the ordinary way. The exact position of every tree, hummock, natural bunker, tracks, hedges, ditches and so on are well defined. The exact areas occupied by permanent pasture, grass grown for hay, crops, clumps of whins, rushes, can all be distinguished in an aerial photograph. These, combined with good ordnance and geological maps, are of inestimable value, and in many cases would assist even the most expert golf architect to make such full use of all the natural features, that thousands of dollars might ultimately be saved in reducing the acreage required, and in minimizing the cost of labour and upkeep.

In these days when manual labour costs so much, it is of supreme importance to reduce it to a minimum by the substitution of mental labour.

Golf architecture is a new art closely allied to that of the artist or sculptor, but also necessitating a scientific knowledge of many other subjects.

In the old days many golf courses were designed by prominent players who after a preliminary inspection of the course simply placed pegs to represent the suggested sites for the tees, greens and bunkers. The whole thing was completed in a few hours and the best results could hardly have been expected, and in fact never were obtained by these methods.

The modern designer, on the other hand, is likely to achieve the most perfect results and make the fullest use of all the natural features by more up-to-date methods.

After a preliminary inspection or inspections, in the calm and quiet of his own study, with an ordnance map, and if possible, aerial photographs in front of him, he can visualize every feature. He is then not so likely to be obsessed by details, but sees everything in perspective and gives it its due value.

He then evolves his scheme and pays a second visit to the ground and, if necessary, modifies his ideas according to the appearance of things on the spot.

In the Victorian era fifty years ago, almost all new golf courses were planned by professionals, and were, incidentally, amazingly bad. They were built up with mathematical precision, a cop bunker extending from the rough on the one side, to the rough on the other, and a similar cop bunker placed for the second shot. There was an entire absence of strategy, interest and excitement except where some natural irremovable object intervened to prevent the designer carrying out his nefarious plans.

Thirty-five years ago I was a member of the Leeds Club which had a course of this description.

The first seven holes were made on flattish ground. The distance of the cop bunkers from the tees at each one measured exactly one hundred and twenty paces, which was the exact distance the professional who planned it thought he could "carry," whatever the direction and strength of the wind might be. Everyone else was to be left out of consideration altogether.

The seventh hole was the only one which was generally admitted to be interesting. There was a magnificent oak tree about a hundred and eighty yards from the tee in a direct line to the hole. This made players think and come to a decision whether they should play to the left, right, or short of it.

The local scratch player considered a hazard in the direct line to the hole, which not infrequently caught his best shots, as most unfair, and insisted on its removal.

The tree was thereupon removed, then the scratch player reversed his views, and said that the hole had become so dull that it was not worth playing. Everyone agreed with him, and so they insisted that some fresh ground should be taken in to make a new hole to take its place. This was found to be impossible unless the previous five holes were scrapped as well.

The committee decided to scrap them and make new holes, so the removal of the tree was the direct cause of the replacement of six holes.

The initial error was due to the fact that the committee had no one to guide or advise them, so they made their own disastrous decision. The result was irremediable except at enormous expense, and unfortunately similar cases arise only too frequently. In these early days, all artificially made inland courses were designed on similar stereotyped lines.

The first person to depart from these principles was the late Mr. John L. Low.

⚔ *Pioneer Architects* ⚔

John L. Low wrote a book over thirty years ago entitled *Concerning Golf,* which was published at the small cost of a shilling (twenty-five cents), and it is still the most illuminating, instructive, and original book written on the subject.

He propounded the principle that no bunker is unfair wherever it is placed. He elaborated his argument and showed how the most fascinating and interesting holes in golf have hazards placed in the exact positions where players would like to go if those hazards were not there.

He illustrates his theme by the end hole bunker on the Old Course at St. Andrews. There is a small deep hazard only about five yards across placed about one hundred and ninety yards from the tee in the direct line for the hole.

John L. Low pointed out that a player has four alternatives: he can play to the left, right, short or over it, and if he gets into it he has only himself to blame, as to say the least he had committed an error of judgment.

This axiom that no bunker is unfair wherever it is placed is the guiding principle of all golf architects.

Some of us would even go further, and say that no hole is a good one unless it has one or more hazards in a direct line to the hole. Max Behr, who is one of the best American golf architects, states that the direct line to the hole is the line of instinct, and that to make a good hole you must break up that direct line in order to create the line of charm.

It was over thirty years ago when John L. Low's ideas were put into practice at Woking, and it was Mr. Stuart Paton who assisted in carrying them out.

I do not remember the exact date of Woking, but in all material respects it remains the same today as it was over thirty years ago.

It is an inland course situated among heather and pine woods, essentially a private club where there are never any important competitions held. It is a difficult course to get at, and still more difficult to be allowed to play unless accompanied by a member.

In consequence, it is not so well known as many of the famous metropolitan courses. Nevertheless it is, from the point of view of strategy and interest, and the undulating character of the greens, more fascinating than any of them.

Mr. H. S. Colt, who was a great friend of John L. Low, held similar ideas. When he was secretary of Sunningdale, he put the ideas into practice, completely revolutionizing this famous course. He altered the long holes and changed entirely the short ones. In doing so he added the necessary strategy and interest, turning it from a dull insipid course into one which was as inspired as the old one had been tedious.

My own interest in golf course architecture originated in an unusual way. During the years of 1899 to 1901 I was serving in the South African war and was much impressed by the way in which a small army of Boers, largely by means of concealed entrenchments, defeated a British army of ten times their numbers.

I considered that their success was due to making the best use of the natural features of the landscape, and by constructing artificial fortifications indistinguishable from natural objects. I came to the conclusion that if similar ideas were developed on scientific lines one could get even better results than the Boers were able to obtain, and following up this idea I made a close study of the subject.

It then struck me that inland courses could be improved in a similar manner by the imitation of the features so characteristic of sand dune courses.

On my return from South Africa I wrote two or three pages in the suggestion book of the Leeds Golf Club, pointing out how the course could be changed by utilizing the natural features, and making others indistinguishable from them and thus creating a greater resemblance to the golf on seaside courses, which in those days everyone admitted to be vastly superior to inland courses, though few, if any, knew why they were better.

USGA

MacKenzie strolling the 1st fairway at St. Andrews.

Not only was little notice taken of my ideas, but when my name was suggested as captain of the club, the committee refused to nominate me, because they said I had such weird ideas regarding golf courses that I would want to alter theirs, bringing in a lot of strange newfangled ideas which must be wrong, as not a single professional in the world agreed with me.

Shortly after this, in 1905, we thought we would attempt to form a new club, so we got together some friends and formed a permanent committee to start Alwoodley Golf Club. The late Mr. Arthur Sykes had also made a close study of golf course architecture, and on putting our heads together we thought we had more chance of getting our ideas through by a permanent committee of friends than by a committee that was changing every year.

On achieving this, we thought that our troubles were over, but in reality they were only just beginning, as every committee meeting was a dog fight, and on many an occasion we nearly came to blows.

At that time Harry Colt made a great success of his alterations at Sunningdale, and two months previously he had got his first fee for advising on alterations at Ganton, a glorious natural course where Harry Vardon was professional.

We managed to persuade the committee to call in Harry Colt to settle the disputes, and he decided in our favour.

The committee agreed to the alterations, but in a few weeks' time such was their conventional outlook they passed resolutions entirely contrary to Harry Colt's and our ideas, and gave us instructions as to how the work was to be carried out during the winter.

As it was an exceedingly wet and unpleasant winter, none of the committee went near the course except Arthur Sykes and myself, so we were able to disregard their views entirely and make the course exactly as we wished. We also had the good fortune to have a greenkeeper, Brown, who was an excellent landscape gardener but who had never seen a golf course before. He had, therefore, no stereotyped ideas, and in consequence fell in with our views. When the

MacKenzie playing the 1st hole at his home course, Alwoodley Golf Club.

course was ready for play in the Spring, the committee came up to view our handiwork, and some of them were furious. They said it was quite unlike any other course and once more we nearly came to blows. In the end they came to an agreement that they would play on it during that summer but that they would alter it during the following winter.

Although there are many things we ourselves, owing to increased experience, would like to change, in no substantial respect has it been altered to this day.

During the last twenty-four years, the committee, except for death or immigration from Leeds, has remained the same as it was the day the club was founded.

Notwithstanding our disputes in the early stages, we would strongly recommend every club to have a permanent committee. It is the only way a policy of continuity can be adopted, and this is particularly important in the case of green committees.

The history of most golf clubs is that a committee is appointed, they make mistakes, and just as they are beginning to learn by these mistakes they resign office and are replaced by others who make still greater mistakes, and so it goes on.

It would be difficult to conceive a better committee than we have at Alwoodley. I cannot refrain from saying that they are such fine sportsmen that they have acknowledged frankly their changed views, and no man could have received greater support and encouragement than I have from them during the last twenty years. I do not know any better club in the world to belong to than Alwoodley.

The committee has always been averse to advertising the course, they will not allow championships there, they discourage competitions and the membership is limited to two hundred men. In consequence of all this I do not remember having to wait more than ten minutes on the first tee.

With the exception of beginners and ladies you rarely hear of anyone taking their score at Alwoodley; they get quite enough fun in trying to beat their doughty opponents and trying to conquer the varied and difficult holes of the course.

Notwithstanding the fact that it has not the natural advantages of many other inland courses—the subsoil consisting of clay—many experts, including Max Behr, think it the best inland course in Britain today.

One of the reasons why Alwoodley, after twenty-five years, has a still more natural appearance than perhaps any other inland course, is that when we were constructing it we were trying to deceive not only the public but also the rest of the committee. We felt that if we could hoodwink them into believing the artificial features we had made were made by Nature we could get away with it and escape their hostile criticism.

The second course I designed was Moortown.

After the success of Alwoodley a group of men, principally consisting of tradespeople, approached me with a view to making a course within a mile of Alwoodley, on ground on which they had obtained a long lease with an option of purchase.

I asked them how much money they had raised for the construction of the course and they informed me one hundred pounds (five hundred dollars).

I told them that they would not be able to make more than one hole for this sum but I thought there was an opportunity of making such a good hole that it would attract new and richer members. They agreed to my suggestion and we made a hole which since then has become world-renowned, namely the eighth or the Gibraltar Hole, as it has come to be known.

The committee took visitors to see it and told them that this was a sample of what the course was going to be like. They said, "This is wonderful," and asked to be put up as members of the club. In this way, sufficient money was obtained to construct the remainder of the course.

Moortown was made about twenty-five years ago, but with the exception of a few new tees and one new bunker it has remained the same up to the present day.

It is true that after the war some new and better players were appointed on to the committee who celebrated their

1929 Ryder Cup. The final day of the matches were the best at Moortown.

Captain Walter Hagen congratulating Captain George Duncan.

election by altering some of the greens and approaches which they considered were unfair. The members, however, arose in their wrath and stated in the most emphatic language that they had taken all the interest and excitement out of these holes and demanded that they should be restored to their original condition. The committee called me in and asked me to restore the holes, so Moortown is today as it was when it was first made.

In the Ryder Cup Match of 1929, the international professionals match between America and Britain, my brother Major C. A. Mackenzie looked after the upkeep of the course.

Notwithstanding several weeks drought it was in excellent order and, when the Ryder Cup Match was played, compared favourably with any British course.

In an article entitled "How to Play Moortown," appearing in several golf papers, it was pointed out that the Thousand Guineas Yorkshire Evening News Competition had been held at Moortown several times, so the British professionals knew the course and had been accustomed to its strategy, but that the American team which had been chosen was so strong the result seemed almost a foregone conclusion. This was by no means the case, as if the Americans did not make a close study of the strategy of Moortown, a similar fate might await them as that which happened to Gene Sarazen in the qualifying round of the Championship at Troon Portland Course.

Troon Portland was, incidentally, one of the courses we had constructed and was far more subtle and required more knowing than the old Troon course.

Every really good golf course should have some touches of subtlety that prevent the golfer doing a low score without much previous practice.

Gene Sarazen ignored the Portland Course in his practice rounds and suffered accordingly.

The Americans were beaten by a narrow margin at Moortown; nevertheless they took their beating in the spirit of true sportsmen and were extremely generous in their praise of the course.

The 6th hole of the new (Portland) course at Troon, Scotland. It was Sarazen's nemesis at the British Open qualifying.

The influence of Alwoodley and Moortown on the popularity of golf in the north of Britain was almost as great as that of Woking and Sunningdale in the south.

Previous to the construction of Alwoodley and Moortown, we were informed by members of Leeds and Headingley clubs that golf was not a popular game in Leeds and that the city could not possibly support a third club.

Leeds and Headingley have been remodeled and have become so popular that they have doubled their membership and since then we have constructed ten new courses within a radius of ten miles from Alwoodley. The last one constructed, Sandmoor, is so popular that it has the largest membership of them all.

These personal reminiscences are given to show the uphill fight which pioneers, and specially those pioneers who had no reputation as players, had in persuading the public to accept what in those days appeared to be revolutionary ideas—ideas which are considered to be self evident truths today.

Personally I was always extraordinarily keen on all kinds of sports and games, but I could never achieve more than a mediocre success in any of them, and so it was quite natural that a member of a committee who, metaphorically speaking, could knock my head off at golf, would assume that his opinion on a debatable point was at any rate of an equal value to mine.

On the other hand what he did not realize, and could hardly be expected to do so, was that I had given the subject years and years of intensive study and thought, whereas he had only given it a few minutes consideration during the time the matter was being debated.

❧ I am as keen as ever on golf, but will always remain an indifferent player. Some years ago I was playing in the final of the Yorkshire Medical Cup. In the first eighteen holes I was up on my opponent, and at the eighth hole of the second round he put two shots out of bounds whilst I was nearly on the green with my second shot. I socketed (shanked) my third to the right of the green, my fourth to the back and my fifth back again nearly to where I had started from. I ultimately lost the hole I seemed certain to win. I continued shanking my shots and lost the match by a heavy margin.

Several friends of mine were looking on, and after the game was over one of them, in a very mysterious and confidential way, buttonholed me and said, "MacKenzie, do you mind me giving you a bit of advice? You are just off to Australia to lay out golf courses. For God's sake don't let them see you play golf or you will never get another job." ❧

John L. Low and Harry Colt were both in the front rank as players, but even they had their troubles.

I am convinced that if Harry Colt had been allowed a free hand at Sunningdale it would have been an even better and more interesting course than it is.

In the long run it is perhaps a good thing for golf that we had these early battles. Looking back, it is amazing how seriously we took our disputes. We fought over them not only at committee meetings but every time we met. The fate of the British Empire might have been at stake.

When the Great War came, how trifling all these things seemed. It is possible, or even probable, that in those early days my own ideas may have been so radical and revolutionary that had I been allowed a free hand the results would have been considered so freakish and so fantastic that there might have been a reaction against them. The criticisms of the Alwoodley Committee undoubtedly had a restraining influence.

The trouble in those early days was that all golfers except a very small handful of pioneers belonged to the penal school. Today we have no such battles to fight. I hardly come across a thinking member of a committee who does not belong to the strategic school.

Owing to the example and the writings of C. B. Macdonald, Max Behr, Robert Hunter, and other able American golf course architects, the United States are absorbing the real sporting spirit of golf so rapidly that today, with the exception of St. Andrews and a few similar clubs, American committees have sounder views than have committees in the "Home of Golf."

Twenty years ago, owing to the influence of John L. Low and other pioneers, new British golf courses were designed by men of education, the professional player having entirely dropped out of the picture. Today, owing to intriguing advertisements, professional players and ex-greenkeepers are again beginning to plan golf courses. Some of them have been able to obtain foremen who have been trained by and worked under the best golf course architects, and they are thus able to construct golf courses which have a superficial resemblance to the real thing. But if one analyzes these recent courses there is a complete absence of variety, strategy, and interest, and a failure in planning them to make the best use of the natural features.

J. F. Abercromby, the architect of Addington, Worplesdon, Coombe Hill and other excellent courses, told me that he was recently called in to advise upon a course of this description.

The committee told him that they wished to convert the course into one of championship rank and asked him how much it would cost.

"How many thousand pounds have you already spent in defacing the landscape?" he asked, "because it will take exactly that amount to restore the natural features you have so ruthlessly destroyed, and then we will discuss the amount it will take to make a championship course."

Some firms who construct golf courses of the type I have been talking about advertise that they are prepared to do the work on a contract basis. This offer always appeals to committees, as they are generally composed of hard headed business men who naturally wish to know the exact cost. Many of them have had experience of the disastrous results, shortly after the war, of constructing buildings on a "cost

One of the many brilliant holes at Addington Golf Club.

plus" basis. They, however, know nothing about golf course architecture. They do not realize that it is essentially different to building operations, and is more closely allied to painting, sculpture, or other kindred arts. They do not know that it is impossible to tie contractors down to exact specifications and quantities.

It is only when work is done in straight lines, angles, and curves, and on stereotyped lines, that specifications can be made.

Anything stereotyped should be avoided on a golf course; all construction work should follow the irregular lines of nature. Any contractor who informs a committee that golf courses can be constructed on contract as they would build a clubhouse is either absolutely ignorant of golf course architecture or is trying to hoodwink the golfing public. It would be just as reasonable to expect an artist to estimate the amount he charges for a painting, according to the quantities of paint and materials he uses.

It is the mental labour which is of paramount importance in any work of art.

You may ask "What safeguard can a committee have in regard to a golf course contract?" and the answer is, "Absolutely none." The contractor can simply pocket as much of the club's money as he chooses and give them what he likes. It is quite possible to construct a golf course by simply gouging eighteen holes in the ground.

As a matter of fact most of the British Championship courses were originally made in this way, and they are vastly better than many other courses which have had hundreds of thousands of dollars expended on them.

I repeat: the value of a golf course is measured by the mental labour put into it, and not by the manual labour and materials. You might specify, for example, that a contractor should construct a couple of hundred bunkers, but the worth of a golf course is not measured in terms of sand traps.

When we advised the Royal Sydney and Australian Golf Clubs, we suggested that they should convert over one hundred sand hazards on each course into grassy hollows, and I do not think we put in more than ten new ones in their place. Since these alterations have been carried out I am informed that these courses have not only become far more pleasurable and interesting but also better tests of golf. Max Behr has succeeded in making better golf courses with a dozen bunkers than any contractor could hope to do with hundreds of them.

After all, the proof of the pudding is in the eating. I do not know of a single first class golf course which has been constructed under contract. And it is interesting to note that not a single one of the famous British and American courses have been made in this way.

A first class architect attempts to give the impression that everything has been done by nature and nothing by himself, whereas a contractor tries to make as big a splash as possible and impress committees with the amount of labour and material he has put into the job.

The International Society of Golf Course Architects (European Section) recognize so strongly that contracts are not to the benefit of the public that they have passed a resolution advising their members not to take them.

It is easy for a club to take effective safeguards in limiting their expenditure on construction work to what they can afford to spend. The smaller the amount they have the more important it is that they should not fritter away their funds in doing bad work which will ultimately have to be scrapped.

❧ Always Aim at "Finality." ❧

Consult a first class architect and tell him frankly that you have only a limited amount to spend and ask him simply to do the essential details and leave the remainder to be done in subsequent years when more funds are available.

In Britain on several occasions we have made the skeleton of a course, which has subsequently become of championship rank, for less than one thousand pounds (five thousand dollars). Even in the early days of such a course the members get a great deal of pleasure out of playing it and watching it improve year by year. Let us assume that in the United States a new club has only $30,000 available to spend on the construction of their course. The architect would first model all the greens with the surrounding bunkers, hillock and hollows. If the sites of the greens were judiciously chosen, this might be done for $10,000 or even less if natural contours were favourable. The seeding would cost $2,000. On the assumption that abundant water were available, the irrigation system could be designed so as to include all the fairways and greens, but for the time being only, the main pipes laid and the greens only supplied with water.

This would cost about $10,000, leaving $8,000 to pay for architect's fees, fertilizers and other necessities. The remainder of the course could be done year by year as more funds became available. Tees are a luxury and can be made at any time with the club's ground staff. If winter rules are put in force, it is not necessary to sow the fairways; the natural vegetation can be mown and rolled until the club can afford to prepare and sow a seeds bed.

The irrigation system of the fairways can also be done afterwards. The featuring, bunkering, drainage and even some of the clearing of the fairways can be postponed to a future date. The important thing is that the skeleton of the course should be right. It can be clothed in future years.

Moortown, where the Ryder Cup match was played in 1929, was, as I have already mentioned, made in this way, and there has never been any alteration to the course. In spite of this it is so good that it compares favourably with any course where the American Championship has been held.

During the first two years of its existence there was never more than five thousand dollars spent on construction work, and yet in the meantime the players got a great deal of fun in attempting to play it.

The natural difficulties also were much greater than on most golf courses. There were no natural grasses, it was covered completely with heather, bushes, rocks, or agricultural crops, and every bit of it had to be drained.

In the case of a building, you cannot stop half way and utilize it before the roof has been put on, the plumbing, heating and interior work done, but as far as a golf course is concerned you can frequently do so. It is necessary, however, that you start with essentials, namely the greens. Other things which, not infrequently, cost three or four times as much, can be left until later. Nevertheless, I would advise that clubs form a subcommittee to check the weekly expenditure and give the architect ample warning to stop before funds show signs of running out.

I am not suggesting that this is the best and wisest way of constructing a golf course. It is at any rate not likely to enhance the reputation of the architect, as visiting golfers in the early stages are only too prone to condemn him for the unfinished condition of the course. When in future years the course becomes first class, people have generally forgotten who the architect was, or attribute the improvement in the course to the club's green committee. On the other hand, the method about which I have been writing is preferable to calling in an inferior architect because his fees are smaller and then finding all the planning is wrong and all the construction is also wrong. A badly routed and planned course can be improved, but it can rarely be made perfect. It is analogous to a badly fitting coat.

Apart from the expense of restoring the natural features which have been ruthlessly destroyed, club members dislike temporary greens, and the partial stoppage of play necessary to re-route and reconstruct their course, but even this is preferable to tinkering with it year after year. Moreover, a course can be reconstructed so rapidly by modern machinery that there is little interference with play.

If a course ever has to be altered, it means that the architect was wrong in the first instance, and yet one sees all over the world golf courses which are being continually altered, and not infrequently the changes that are made are no great improvement on the old holes.

36

It is often suggested that changes in the ball may necessitate alterations to the course, but this is nonsense. A well-designed golf course should suit any golf ball or any class of player. The Old Course at St. Andrews is a classical example. It was the best in the days of the feather, guttie, and the Haskell ball, and Bobby Jones still describes it as the best today.

There are many golf course architects who have never had a golf course altered when they have been given a free hand to carry out their ideas in the first place. I do not think that J. F. Abercromby, Harry Colt or Max Behr have ever had a course altered.

None of our courses in America have ever been changed, and moreover in one case only have we exceeded the sum allotted to us in the construction of a course.

In the United States, golf courses are becoming more and more perfect. American golfers owe a debt of gratitude to Charles Blair Macdonald, who was not only the first United States Amateur Champion but the father of golf architecture in America.

He had an uphill fight in educating American golfers to an appreciation of a really good golf course. On the National Golf Links, Lido, and other links he made copies of famous holes of the old British Championship courses, which was an expensive way of constructing golf courses, but probably the only means of combating criticism and familiarizing players with real golf. One learns by bitter experience how difficult it is to escape hostile criticism when one makes a hole of the adventurous type.

Even good golfers at first sight look upon holes of this kind as unfair. Witness, for example, Bobby Jones' earliest impressions of St. Andrews. In an article written some time ago for the *British Sporting and Dramatic* he describes the history of his first impressions of the Old Course at St. Andrews in a most fascinating and interesting manner. He frankly admits that at first sight he considered it was the most unfair and one of the worst courses he had ever played on. Then in a vivid word picture, he describes how he changed his

USGA

Bobby Jones at St. Andrews, his favorite course.

views and why, today, not only does he consider it the best course in the world, but he states that he gets more pleasure out of playing it than a hundred other golf courses.

A first class hole must have subtleties and strategic problems which are difficult to understand, and are therefore extremely likely to be condemned at first sight by even the best players. One can only escape hostile criticism by pointing out that a hole is a copy of such and such a hole like "the Road," "Eden," "Redan" or some other equally famous.

It was in this way that Macdonald was able to familiarize American players with real golf and make the work easy for other architects that followed him.

⚔ *"Kolfen"* ⚔

It was Charles Blair Macdonald who, in his interesting book *Scotland's Gift—Golf* effectively disproved the theory that the Dutch game Kolfen was the origin of golf. He points out that it was played on the ice, only one club was used and the objective was not a hole in the ground. The Dutch game more closely resembled hockey, or as it is called in Scotland, "shinty."

MacKenzie and Hunter on one of their best—and one of the world's best par 3's ever built—the 16th hole at Cypress Point.

40

❖2❖
General Principles

Twenty years ago I published in the English paper *Golfing* a series of articles on what I considered the ideal golf course. Later on these were reprinted in my little book, *Golf Architecture.*

As the essence of golf is variety, it would not be wise to be too didactic as to what does constitute the ideal golf course, but my suggestions for it would be very much on the lines of what I wrote twenty years ago, and as I can hardly improve on that, I set it down here as it was originally written.

1. The course, where possible, should be arranged in two loops of nine holes.
2. There should be a large proportion of good two-shot holes, and at least four one-shot holes.
3. There should be little walking between the greens and tees, and the course should be arranged so that in the first instance there is always a slight walk forwards from the green to the next tee; then the holes are sufficiently elastic to be lengthened in the future if necessary.
4. The greens and fairways should be sufficiently undulating, but there should be no hill climbing.

5. Every hole should be different in character.
6. There should be a minimum of blindness for the approach shots.
7. The course should have beautiful surroundings, and all the artificial features should have so natural an appearance that a stranger is unable to distinguish them from nature itself.
8. There should be a sufficient number of heroic carries from the tee, but the course should be arranged so that the weaker player with the loss of a stroke, or portion of a stroke, shall always have an alternate route open to him.
9. There should be infinite variety in the strokes required to play the various holes—that is, interesting brassie shots, iron shots, pitch and run up shots.
10. There should be a complete absence of the annoyance and irritation caused by the necessity of searching for lost balls.
11. The course should be so interesting that even the scratch man is constantly stimulated to improve his game in attempting shots he has hitherto been unable to play.
12. The course should be so arranged that the long handicap player or even the absolute beginner should be able to enjoy his round in spite of the fact that he is piling up a big score. In other words the beginner should not be continually harassed by losing strokes from playing out of sand bunkers. The layout should be so arranged that he loses strokes because he is making wide detours to avoid hazards.
13. The course should be equally good during winter and summer, the texture of the greens and fairways should be perfect and the approaches should have the same consistency as the greens.

❧ *A Decided Advantage* ❧

In regard to the first three principles there can be little difference of opinion. It is a considerable advantage that a course should be arranged in two loops of nine holes, as on a busy day players can commence at either the first or the tenth tee. On the other hand one can easily sacrifice the best features of good golfing land by being too insistent on this principle.

I believe I was the first to write articles emphasizing the importance of the two loops of nine holes.

During recent years in the United States I have had more sleepless nights owing to committees being obsessed by this principle than anything else, and I have often regretted that it had ever been propounded.

If land for a golf course lends itself readily to constructing the two loops, well and good, but it is a great mistake to sacrifice excellent natural features for the purpose of obtaining it. Most of the world's best known courses, such as nearly all the British Championship courses, The National, Pine Valley, Cypress Point, Pebble Beach, and many others I could name, are without loops. There is a charm in exploring fresh country and never seeing the same view twice until one arrives back at the clubhouse.

In regard to the fourth principle, it used to be a common fallacy that greens were to be made dead flat. Even on some of the best golf courses at the present day you find them made like croquet lawns. There has been somewhat of a reaction lately against undulating greens, but this, I believe, is entirely due to the fact that the undulations have been made of a wrong character, composed either of finicky little humps or of the "ridge and furrow" type. Natural undulations are the exact opposite of the artificial ridge and furrow. The latter has a narrow hollow and a broad ridge, whereas the former has a large, bold sweeping hollow and a narrow ridge.

The most interesting putting course I have ever seen is the Ladies' Putting Course at St. Andrews. Even first class golfers consider it a privilege to be invited there and are to be found putting with the greatest enthusiasm from early morning till late at night. There the undulations are of the boldest possible type—large sweeping hollows rising abruptly four to five feet or more to small plateaus. A modern architect who

Tom Doak

The Ladies' Putting Course at St. Andrews. Golfers are found here putting from early morning to late at night with the greatest enthusiasm.

dared to reproduce the boldness of these St. Andrews undulations could hardly hope to escape hostile criticism.

In constructing natural looking undulations, one should attempt to study the manner in which those among sand dunes are formed. These are fashioned by the wind blowing up the sand in the form of waves which have become gradually turfed over in the course of time. Natural undulations are therefore of a similar shape to the waves one sees by the seashore and are of all sorts of shapes and sizes, but are characterized by the fact that the hollows between the waves are broader than the waves themselves. If undulations are made like this there are always plenty of comparatively flat places

44

where the greenkeeper can put the flag, and there should never be any necessity to cut a hole in the slope.

A test of a good undulation is that it should be easy to use a mowing machine over it. If undulations are made of the kind I describe, it is hardly possible to make them too bold or too large. Perhaps the most irritating type of undulation is the finicky little hump or side slope which you do not see until after you have missed your putt and then begin to wonder why it has not gone into the hole.

An almost equally common delusion is that fairways should be flat. I quite agree that there is nothing worse than a fairway on a severe side slope, but, on the other hand, there are few things more monotonous than playing every shot from a dead flat fairway. The unobservant player never seems to realize that one of the chief charms of the best seaside links is the undulating fairways such as those near the clubhouse at Deal, Sandwich, and, most of all, at the Old Course at St. Andrews, where the ground is a continual roll from the first tee to the last green and where one never has the same shot to play twice over. On these fairways one hardly ever has a level stance or lie. It is this that makes the variety of a seaside course, and variety in golf is everything.

During recent years I was under the impression that all golf critics realized the importance of undulating fairways, but during the last Walker Cup Match at Sandwich I was horrified to find a Chicago man writing to his paper and saying that Sandwich would be an excellent course if it were not for the unfair undulations of the fairways. It is true that Sandwich is badly designed, constructed and bunkered, but the magnificent bold, sweeping undulations which, with the exception of some on the greens, have so far escaped destruction by the hand of man, put it in a class vastly superior to most American inland courses.

All the British Championship courses owe their interest to their undulations.

If, for example, one considers St. Andrews hole by hole, it is surprising to find at how many of them the dominating and important incident is associated with an insignificant-

An undulating fairway at St. Andrews that provides all players variety and challenge.

Tom Doak

looking hollow or bank often running obliquely to your line of approach. In constructing undulations of this kind on inland courses it is well to make them with as much variety as possible and in the direction you wish the player to go, and to keep the fairways comparatively flat so as to encourage players to place their shots and thus get in a favourable position for their next.

In this connection plasticine is often used for making models of undulations. Plasticine is useful to teach the greenkeeper points in construction he would not otherwise understand; in fact I believe I was the first golf course designer to use it for this purpose. The 14th green at Alwoodley, which was the first one made there, was constructed from a model in plasticine. It has its disadvantages, however, as a course constructed entirely from models in plasticine always has an artificial appearance and can never be done as cheaply as one in which the superintendent is allowed a comparatively free hand in modeling the undulations in such a manner that not only do they harmonize with their surroundings but are constructed according to the various changes in the subsoil discovered whilst doing the work.

A green constructed from a model in plasticine looks like a plasticine model. One of the reasons for this is that it is difficult to produce the hollows in plasticine as well as the rises. Many architects have, with increasing experience, given it up in favour of sketches.

Tom Simpson, the architect of Chiberta and other excellent courses, has got far better results since he gave up using it. It was Tom Simpson, I think, who discovered to his own astonishment, that he was a born artist. Some of his sketches are very well done and are most impressive.

❈ *Fashions in Golf Course Architecture* ❈

In regard to the fifth principle—that every hole should have a different character—a common mistake is to follow prevailing fashions. At first we had the artificial cop bunkers extending in a dead straight line from the rough on the one side to the rough on the other; in modern course architecture these are fortunately extinct. Then we had the fashion of pot bunkers running down each side of the course. This was, if anything, an even more objectionable type of golf than the last. Thirdly, we have had what has been called the "alpinisation" of golf courses.

In this connection I would point out that constructors should be careful not to make hillocks so high in the direct line to the hole that they block out the view; a little to one side of the bee line they may be made as high as one pleases, but in the direct line hollows should, as a rule, take the place of hillocks.

This is the exact opposite to what is found on many golf courses where the hollows are at the sides and the banks in the middle. The great thing in constructing a golf course is to ensure variety and make everything look natural. The greatest compliment that can be paid to a constructor is for players to think his artificial work is natural. On Alwoodley and Moortown practically every green and every hummock has been artificially made, yet it is difficult to convince a stranger that this is so. I remember a chairman of a green committee of one of the best known clubs in the north of England telling me that it would be impossible to make their course anything like Alwoodley, as there we had such a wealth of natural hollows, hillocks, and undulations. It was only with great difficulty that I was able to persuade him that, to use an Irishism, these natural features which he so much admired had all been created artificially. I have even heard one of the members of the Alwoodley green committee telling a well-known writer on golf that the hummocks surrounding one of the greens had always been there; he himself had forgotten that he had been present when the site for them was pegged out.

❧ Blind Holes ❧

It is not nearly as common an error to make blind holes as it was in days gone by. A blind tee shot may be forgiven, or a full shot to the green on a seaside course, when the greens can usually be located accurately by the position of the surrounding hummocks, but an approach shot should never be blind, as this prevents an expert player, except by a fluke, from placing his approach so near the hole that he gets down in one putt.

Blind holes on an inland course where there are no sandhills to locate the green should never be permitted, but an even more annoying form of blindness is that which is so frequently found on inland courses: that is, when the flag is visible but the surface of the green cannot be seen. On a green of this description no one can possibly tell whether the flag is at the front, in the middle or at the back of the green and it is particularly irritating to play your shot expecting to find it "dead" and then to discover that your ball is at least twenty yards short.

On a seaside course there may be a certain amount of pleasurable excitement in running up to the top of a hillock in the hope of seeing your ball near the flag, but this is a kind of thing of which one gets rather tired as one grows older.

❧ Importance of Beauty ❧

Another erroneous idea which is prevalent is that beauty does not matter on a golf course. One often hears players say they "don't care a tinker's cuss" about their surroundings, what they want is good golf. One of the best known writers on golf has been jeering at architects for attempting to make beautiful bunkers. If he prefers ugly bunkers, ugly greens, and ugly surroundings generally, he is welcome to them, but I do not think for an instant that he believes what he is writing about, for at the same time he talks about the beauties of the natural courses. The chief object of every golf architect or greenkeeper worth his salt is to imitate the beauties of nature so closely as to make his work indistinguishable from Nature herself.

I have not the slightest hesitation in saying that beauty means a great deal on a golf course; even the man who emphatically states that he does not care a hang for beauty is subconsciously influenced by his surroundings. A beautiful hole appeals not only to the short but also to the long handicap player, and there are few first rate holes which are not at the same time, either in the grandeur of their undulations and hazards, or the character of their surroundings, things of beauty in themselves.

⊁ It is not suggested that we should all play around the links after the manner of the curate playing with the deaf old Scotsman. The curate was audibly expressing his admiration of the scenery, the greens and everything in general until they finally arrived at a green surrounded by a rookery. The curate remarked "Is it not delightful to hear the rooks?" "What's that?" said the deaf old Scottie. "Is it not delightful to hear the rooks?" reiterated the curate. The Scotsman shook his head in disgust "I canna hear-r a wor-r-d you're saying for those dommed craws," he replied. ⊁

The finest courses in existence are natural ones. Such courses as St. Andrews, and the championship courses generally, are admitted to provide a fine test of golf. It is by virtue of their natural formation that they do so. The beauty of golf courses in the past has suffered from the creations of ugly and unimaginative design. Square, flat greens and geometrical bunkers have not only been an eyesore upon the whole landscape, but have detracted from the infinite variety of play which is the heritage of the game.

My reputation in the past has been based on the fact that I have endeavored to conserve the existing natural features and, where these were lacking, to create formations in the spirit of nature herself. In other words, while always keeping uppermost the provision of a splendid test of golf, I have striven to achieve beauty.

It may at first appear unreasonable that the question of aesthetics should enter into golf course design. However, on deeper analysis it becomes clear that the great courses, and in detail all the famous holes and greens, are fascinating to the golfer by reason of their shape, their situation and the character of their modeling. When these elements obey the fundamental laws of balance, of harmony and fine proportion, they give rise to what we call beauty. This excellence of design is more felt than fully realized by the players, but nevertheless it is constantly exercising a subconscious influence upon him and in course of time he grows to admire such a course as all works of beauty must be eventually felt and admired.

❧ Cypress Point ❧

The most beautiful of all courses we have made is Cypress Point, and at the same time it is also the most difficult of all our courses. When we constructed Cypress Point we expected we should be snowed under by hostile criticism.

My experience of really first class holes is that, like the famous "Road Hole" at St. Andrews, they at first sight excite the most violent spirit of antagonism. It is only after the holes have been played many times that the feeling of resentment disappears and the former critics become the strongest supporters.

More than half the holes at Cypress Point were of such a nature that I knew by experience that they would at first

MacKenzie about to play the most photographed hole in golf.

sight be characterized as unfair. They were so subtle and had such difficult strategic problems that I knew even the best players could not hope to make a good score except after considerable practice. I was not present when the course was opened for play, but my late partner, Robert Hunter, wrote to me and said, "Everyone without exception thinks that Cypress Point is the best in the United States. There is not a word of hostile criticism."

My reply was to write back and ask him what was wrong with it. I had been so accustomed to having our best holes torn to pieces that I was actually disturbed at the lack of criticism. I now believe that Cypress Point has escaped criticism simply because it is so incomparably beautiful. All the artificial features are so natural in appearance that it is difficult to believe they have been made by the hand of man.

Apart from the golf, it is the only course I know where one literally gasps with astonishment at its beauty. Cypress Point bears out my contention that every man is subconsciously influenced by beauty and that the construction of artificial features indistinguishable from the finest things in nature is the surest way to disarm criticism.

⋊ *The Real Object of a Hazard* ⋉

Many of the remaining principles depend on the proper disposition of hazards, and I have a rather wider definition of hazards than is given by the rules of the golf committee. As a minor kind of hazard, undulating ground, hummocks and hollows might be included.

Most golfers have an erroneous view of the real object of hazards. The majority of them simply look upon a hazard as a means of punishing a bad shot, whereas their real object is to make the game more interesting. The attitude of the ordinary golfer towards hazards may be illustrated by the following tale, which I have frequently told before but which will well bear repeating.

⊀ A player visiting a Scottish course asked his caddie what the members thought of a stream which was winding in and out between several of the holes. The caddie replied "Weel, we've got an old Scottish major here who, when he gets ower it says 'Weel ower the bonnie wee burn ma laddie' but when he gets into it he says 'Pick ma ball oot o' thot domned sewer'." ⊁

I was once playing with my brother, who was home on leave from abroad. He was clearly enjoying his game, but at Alwoodley we have one solitary pond into which he topped three balls. On arriving back at the clubhouse he was asked how he liked the course. His only remark about it was, "You've got too many ruddy ponds about." The use of a water hazard is a very debatable question. Being a Scotsman, I am naturally opposed to water in its undiluted state. I am also opposed to a hazard involving the risk of a lost ball.

On the other hand, I am very much in favour of utilizing water where it exists as a natural feature, particularly if there is a clean bottom and there is a chance of recovering one's ball. Players also get such a tremendous thrill driving over the ocean at the spectacular 16th and 17th holes at Cypress Point that this also is well worth the risk of losing a ball or two. I recently crossed over from England with an American who told me that the 16th at Cypress Point had cost him a fortune in golf balls, as he would always play for the long carry to the green across the ocean, but the joy of seeing his ball land on the green and the feeling of something achieved when it did so was worth all the balls he put into the ocean in his attempts to drive the hazard.

I find committees who are amazingly inconsistent with regard to water hazards. On four different occasions in one year I have been asked to create, at enormous expense, an artificial lake where there was none existing, and on other occasions when I have been constructing courses, those in authority have asked me to keep as far away as possible from magnificent natural lakes.

I often find committees desiring me to culvert a clear stream which is a thing of great beauty and where there is no risk of losing one's ball, and yet on other occasions I am requested to construct a ditch as a hazard when the soil is of such a nature that there is no hope, except at great expense, of obtaining clear water where one can find a ball which goes into the hazard.

Given a free hand, I would use an existing water hazard to the fullest possible extent, but I am very much opposed to creating artificial ones at a cost of thousands of dollars when the money can be used to give much greater thrills in some other way.

It is much too large a subject to go into the question of the placing of hazards, but I would like to emphasize a fundamental principle, which is, as has already been pointed out, that no hazard is unfair wherever it is placed. A hazard placed in the exact position where a player would naturally go is frequently the most interesting situation, as a special effort is then needed to get over it or to avoid it.

❧ Give the Player Thrills ❧

One of the objects in placing hazards is to give the players as much pleasurable excitement as possible. On many inland courses there is not a thrill on the whole round, and yet on some of the British Championship courses one rarely takes a club out of the bag without having an interesting shot to play. This particularly applies to the Old Course at St. Andrews, and is one of the reasons why it always retains its popularity with all classes of players. It is quite true that even this course is condemned by some, but this may be due to the fact that they have not brains enough, or have not played it long enough, to appreciate its many virtues.

There are some leading players who honestly dislike the dramatic element in golf. They hate anything which is likely to interfere with a constant succession of threes and fours. They look upon everything in the "card and pencil spirit."

The average club member on the other hand is a keen sportsman who looks upon golf in the "spirit of adventure," and that is why St. Andrews and courses modeled on similar ideals appeal to him.

No one would pretend that the Old Course at St. Andrews was perfect. It has its disadvantages, particularly in the absence of long carries from the tee and in its blind bunkers, but no links in the world grows upon all classes of players in the same manner. The longer one plays there the keener one gets, and this is a much truer test of a good course than one which pleases at first and is boring later on.

A good golf course is like good music or good anything else: it is not necessarily a course which appeals the first time one plays over it, but one which grows on the player the more frequently he visits it.

St. Andrews is a standing example of the possibility of making a course which is pleasurable to all classes of golfers, not only to the thirty handicap players but to the plus fourteen man if there ever was or will be such a person.

It is an interesting fact that few hazards are of any interest which are out of what is known to medical men as the direct field of vision. This does not extend much further than ten to twenty yards on either side of the direct line to the hole. Hazards placed outside these limits are usually of little interest, and are simply a source of irritation.

Hazards should be placed with an object in mind, and not one should be made which has not some influence on the line of play to the hole.

❧ I recently visited a course in Montreal, a magnificent piece of golfing country with beautiful surroundings called Mount Bruno. I had seen it the previous year when I played there with the British Senior Golfers team. In the interim they had constructed a new bunker a long way off the line on the right of the fairway. I asked them what it was for and they said "to punish a bad slice." I remarked "Good Lord, if a man slices as badly as that you should be sorry for him." ❧

This course was much too difficult for the "dub" and the old gentleman, but was of no earthly interest to a player like Bobby Jones. The green committee were anxious that we should reconstruct it, but the directors thought we would make it too difficult and turned the proposition down. They little knew that the modern golf architect would wipe out all the penal hazards and make it much easier but at the same time more interesting and pleasurable to all classes of players.

The chairman of the green committee of Lake Merced Golf Course reminded me the other day that although we had scrapped one hundred and forty bunkers on their course we had made it a far finer test of golf and incidentally saved the whole cost of the reconstruction in reduced maintenance costs every year.

❧ *Bunkers* ❧

On many courses there are far too many bunkers. The sides of the fairways are riddled with them, and many of the courses would be equally interesting and infinitely more pleasurable if half the bunkers were turfed over and converted into grassy hollows.

It is often possible to make a hole sufficiently interesting with one or two bunkers at the most.

For example, it is obvious from the diagram that the green guarding bunker B has a considerable influence on the line of play to the hole. The longer the carry a player achieves over the stream the easier his second shot becomes. If it were not for this bunker, not only the approach but the tee shot would be uninteresting, as there would be no object in essaying the long carry across the stream.

Many poor golf courses are made in an endeavor to eliminate the element of luck. You can no more eliminate luck in golf than you can in cricket, and in neither case is it possible to punish every bad shot. If you succeeded in doing

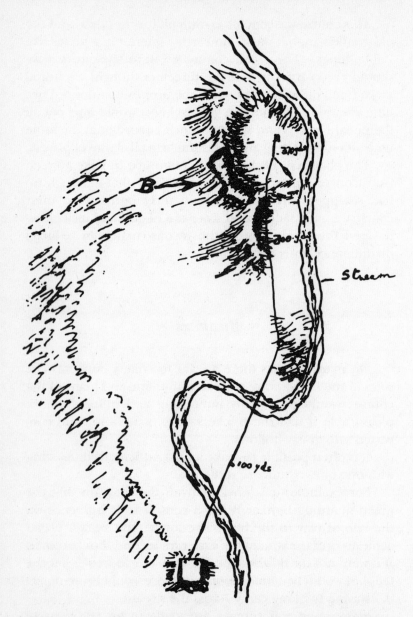

370 yards, par 4. Illustrating the value of one bunker (B). Any additional bunker for the tee shot or across the approach to the green would materially lessen the interest of the hole. The moral is: "Few bunkers placed in interesting positions!"

so you would only make both games uninteresting and no one would want to play them.

There are many points of resemblance between cricket and golf. The fielders in cricket correspond to the hazards in golf. They are placed in the positions where the majority of shots go, and obviously it should be easier with a stationary ball to avoid the hazards than to play a fast bowled ball at cricket to avoid the fielders. In both games it is only a proportion of the bad shots that get punished, but notwithstanding this the man who is playing the best game invariably comes out on top.

It is an important thing in golf to make holes look much more difficult than they really are. People get more pleasure in doing a hole which looks almost impossible and yet is not so difficult as it appears.

In this connection it may be pointed out that rough grass is of little interest as a hazard. It is frequently much more difficult than a fearsome looking bunker or belt of whin bushes or rushes, but it causes considerable annoyance in lost balls, and no one ever gets the same thrill in driving over a stretch of rough as over a spectacular bunker, although in reality a bunker many not be so severe.

Narrow fairways bordered by long grass make bad golfers. They do so by destroying the harmony and continuity of the game and in causing a stilted and a cramped style, destroying all freedom of play.

There is no defined line between fairways at the great schools of golf like St. Andrews or Hoylake. It is a common error to cut rough in straight lines, whereas it ought to be cut in irregular natural-looking curves. The fairways should gradually widen out where the long drive goes. In this way a long driver is given a little more latitude for pulling or slicing. Moreover, irregular curves assist a player in locating the exact position of a ball which has left the fairway and entered the rough.

It is even better to simply keep irregular islands of rushes, bents, whins, patches of fescues, and so on, and to do away entirely with clover and all luxuriant grasses which involve any risk of losing a ball.

Rough grass is of no value for protecting danger points; it has no effect in keeping people straight, but merely prolongs the length of time players are in the danger zone.

Charles Ambrose, an able golfer, writer, artist, and critic, has recently been advocating that the proper way to limit the flight of the golf ball is to penalize everyone who drives over a certain distance, leaving rough grass so as to make them drive into a bottleneck. This might be permissible on one or two holes, like the first at Prestwick or the ninth at Cypress Point, but would be absolutely wrong if repeated several times. The point naturally arises of where Charles Ambrose would make his bottleneck. If he took a point beyond which he usually drives, then a gale of wind or a period of drought causing a greater run of the ball would destroy all his calculations and he himself would then be caught driving into the bottleneck.

Experience has taught us that it is most unsafe to generalize on length. Even a mild breeze with or against the player may make fifty or a hundred yards difference in the length of the flight of a ball. I remember seeing the professionals playing at Alwoodley during one of the few competitions held there. On the first day there was a strong gale of wind against the players and on the fourth hole they were taking three full shots with wood. On the second day the wind had completely veered round and some of them were reaching the green with a drive and mashie-niblick.

❧ *Flight of the Ball* ❧

On the other hand I am a strong believer in limiting the flight of the ball. Pleasure in obtaining length is only a matter of relativity. One got quite as much fun in driving the old Haskell ball twenty yards further than one's opponent as today one gets in hitting the small heavy ball twenty yards further. Quite as big a thrill is obtained in hitting a baseball or cricket ball a hundred yards as a golf ball two hundred.

One of the difficulties with which we have to contend is that any marked limitation of the flight of the ball is certain to be unpopular for some time after its inauguration. Golfers would dislike to find that they were unable to carry a bunker they were formerly able to do. They would feel as though they had suddenly grown old.

Something very drastic ought to have been done years and years ago. Golf courses are becoming far too long. Twenty years ago we played three rounds of golf a day and considered we had taken an interminably long time if we took more than two hours to play a round. Today it not infrequently takes over three hours.

The U.S.G.A are on the right lines but they have not gone far enough. They ought to have standardized a floater. It is a much pleasanter ball to play with than any other. The bigger the ball the pleasanter it is to hit, and it also sits up better on the fairway and is more easily picked up with a wooden club. Long hitters today rarely play wood except off the tee, and a floater would bring back again all the pleasures of wooden shot play. There is little difference in the length obtained with wood when playing a floater or a small heavy ball, but the small ball flies much further off an iron club so there is little necessity to use a wood. The desirability of a still further limitation of the flight of the golf ball is purely a question of what is going to give lasting pleasure to the greatest number. I remember many years ago in the days of the gutty getting hold of two of the first Haskell balls that came to Scotland. With the aid of the Haskell I was able to outdrive opponents who formerly outdrove me. This gave me a temporary delight, but it only lasted up to the time that they were able to obtain the rubber cored balls.

Similarly, today many are trying to obtain a temporary advantage by buying the latest far-flying ball on the market. It is often suggested that we have already got to the limit of flight of a golf ball. I do not believe it, as there is no limit to science. During the war, experts told us we had got to the

61

limit of flight of a cannonball; then the Germans invented a gun which propelled a shell three times as far as it had ever been sent before.

The Royal and Ancient "rules of golf" committee intimate that they will put a stop to any new ball which flies appreciably further, but the difficulty is how can they? There may not be any sudden change which would warrant them intervening. On the other hand I feel sure that during the last few years improvements have been made in the manufacture of golf balls which enable them to fly two or three yards further every year. I have recently been playing with the new English ball for which the manufacturers claim that it will fly twelve yards further than any other. I believe their claim to be a true one. We have already got to the stage when there is too much walking and too little golf.

Strange to say the opposition to a drastic limitation in the flight of the golf ball comes from the short drivers. They would, in relation to the long driver, benefit the most.

I understand that when tests were made with a ball testing machine of the small ball against the large one there was fifteen yards difference in flight when the machine was adjusted to send the small ball 250 yards but only five yards when it was adjusted to send it 200. Therefore, the larger the ball the less relative advantage gained by a long hitter.

I am firmly convinced that a floater would, in the long run, give more lasting pleasure. It would restore much of the old finesse and skill of the game. In the old days it was a joy to watch a skillful player like Harold Hilton juggling with a golf ball. He would play a low shot into the wind or a high ball when the wind was in his favour. When the wind was from the right he would play into it with a pull so that he would get its help. If on the other hand the wind blew from the left he would play into it with a slice.

A floater would also make for much greater variety and interest in approaching. Today nearly everyone plays a coarse and vulgar pitch which punches a hole in the green. With the exception of the Old Course at St. Andrews and few similar courses, there is rarely any necessity to play any other kind of shot. Golfers are losing the joy of playing the variety of approach shots that were so necessary in the old days.

There is little the golf architect can do to remedy this except to point out from his experience and knowledge of psychology what is likely to give the greatest enjoyment to the greatest number. It has been suggested that a limitation of the flight of the golf ball may necessitate an alteration to golf courses, but this is not the case, as a good golf course, to quote once more St. Andrews Old Course, should be first class for every ball and every conceivable class of player.

I wrote this before the new standard U.S.G.A. larger ball had come into general use, but I am convinced that after the initial prejudice against any new thing has been overcome it will be welcomed by the majority of players. This will make things easier for the "rules of golf committee" to go a step further and introduce the floater. A floater will be a much more pleasurable ball to play with, but it is possible and even probable that even this may not solve our problem of restricting the flight of the ball.

There is nothing to prevent some inventive genius coming along and devising a method of making it still more resilient and increasing its length of flight. As I said before, there is no limit to science. Would it not be possible, although I admit practical difficulties might arise, to legislate so that every known make of ball has to conform to tests of a ball testing machine? Or in other words, every ball which flew further than the prescribed length would be automatically rejected.

It is well that the minds of the golfing public should be clarified in connection with the problem of restricting the flight of the ball, and the pros and cons regarding the introduction of a restricted floater ball may be summarized as follows.

1. To a certain extent, the larger the ball the more pleasurable it is to hit.
2. It would restore a greater amount of wooden play because

a large ball sits up more readily on the fairway and because, relatively to a small ball, a larger ball flies much further off a wooden club than an iron. Moreover, with the exception of a ribbed iron, a controlled slice or pull shot can be more readily played with a wood than an iron.

3. It would help to restore the joy of playing the variety of approach shots so necessary in the olden days, e.g., approach shots with topspin running over hill and through dale, shots with spring from left to right or right to left which would help to save us from the same monotonous pitch played time after time.

4. It would save us from the tiring backward walks from greens to tees in the effort to obtain more length, destroying the interest and the strategy of the holes.

5. It would enable water hazards to be used more often, as players would not be subjected to the expense and annoyance of losing balls in the water.

6. For obvious reasons it would lessen the cost of golf and make the game more democratic.

The only objection I can see to limiting the flight of the ball is a purely temporary one. Players at first sight would dislike driving an appreciably shorter distance than they had been accustomed to. They would, however, soon get over this when they found their usual opponents were similarly limited, and particularly when they found they got more golf with less walking.

The pleasure of hitting a larger ball two hundred yards would be just as great or even greater than hitting a smaller one two hundred and twenty. This objection could also be eliminated to a great extent by putting the tees forward.

In arguments regarding the floater ball, the remark is often made that the present regulations permit you to use a floater ball if you prefer it. Some of us do use it. Nevertheless it is not quite the same thing playing with it against opponents who are using the small ball and outdriving you in consequence. As far as I personally am concerned, I am being consistently outdriven by my friends, so a few yards more or less makes little difference, and I find the extra fun in playing the shots with a floater more than compensates for any loss of distance.

The type of ball used has a considerable influence on the principles underlying golf architecture, but not by any means to the extent some people believe. Another strong influence is the type of clubs which are used. The ribbed club had a detrimental effect on the skill necessary in playing a golf course, and it was all to the good of golf that the rules of golf committee barred it.

It was stated that one American who won a British Championship had six niblicks of varying lofts. Surely this sort of thing is not to the good of golf.

In the old days Johnny Ball, 8-time British Amateur Champion, frequently played with two clubs only and played as well as anyone else with a complete bagful of ironmongery. I would like to see the rules of golf committee restrict golfers to the use of six clubs.

Players might be permitted to choose any six they like. A driver, a brassie, iron, mashie, niblick and putter should be enough for anyone, and it would, incidentally, make the game more democratic. Why should a player get an extra advantage because of extra wealth? In addition to Charles Ambrose, Roger Wethered, Sr. and Tom Simpson have also advocated that the efforts of the ball manufacturers to increase the flight of the golf ball should be neutralized by penalizing anyone who drives too far.

It might be quite reasonable for the sake of variety and to force players to use their heads to do this at one or two holes, but I can hardly imagine anything more unfair than to have many holes of this type. Moreover, in actual practice it would probably penalize the short driver's second shot when he was shooting against the wind to an even greater extent than the long driver's first shot. After all, long driving is not a crime—it is a virtue and is more frequently achieved by skill and grace of motion than by mere brute force. Long drivers should be rewarded, and as a general rule they should have greater latitude, and not less, than short drivers.

I have already said that long grass is of little interest as a hazard. On the other hand, undulating ground consisting of hillocks and hollows is of enormous interest. In fact, the interest of the British Championship courses, which are still the most fascinating in the world, consists almost entirely in the natural hillocks and hollows.

Hummocks and hollows should be made all sorts of different shapes and sizes and should have a natural appearance with plenty of slope at the bottom, like large waves. Most of the hummocks and hollows should be so smooth that the mowing machine can be used over them, and the glorified molehills one sees on so many courses should be avoided.

Bunkers on an inland course should, as a rule, be made in the opposite way to what is customary. At the present time most bunkers have the hollows sanded and the banks turfed. You get a much more natural appearance, however, if the hollows are partly turfed over and the hummocks sanded. This has many advantages. The appearance is more like a seaside course; the sand, being above the level of the ground, always remains dry; the contrast between white or yellow sand and the grass helps one to judge distances much more accurately and enable the ball to be found more easily, while the great disadvantage and expense of scything the long grass on the hummocks to prevent lost balls is entirely done away with.

Ordinary bunkers, as a rule, are made in quite the wrong way. The face is usually too upright and the ball gets into an unplayable position under the face. The bottom of the bank of a bunker should have a considerable slope so that a ball always rolls toward the middle. The top of a bunker may, as it usually does in nature, be made to overhang a little so that a topped ball may be prevented from running through it.

Experience gained in the imitation of natural slopes in bunker making was ultimately responsible for saving tens of thousands of pounds in revetting material in the Great War. Trenches with sides made like the banks of a stream with a considerable slope at the bottom remained standing without any revetting material. Before this principle was pointed out soldiers invariably dug their trenches with a slope at the top, and as they got further down the sides became more vertical and sometimes even undercut. A trench of this kind invariably fell in, whereas those made vertical at the top with the slope at the bottom did not do so.

During recent years I have attempted to make bunkers with alternate routes out of them, or in other words, parts of the banks only—as in nature—should overhang. In other places the slopes should be so gradual that a putter can be used out of them, but not as a rule in a direct line to the hole.

As a rule, hazards are placed too far away from the green they are intended to guard. They should be placed immediately on the edge of the green and then, particularly if they are in the form of smooth hillocks and hollows, the player who is wide of them has an extremely difficult pitch and is frequently worse off than the man who is among them.

A bunker eating into a green is by far the most equitable way of giving a golfer full advantage for accurate play. It not only penalizes the man who is in it but also everyone who is wide of it. For example, a player who is in the "Road bunker" at the seventeenth at St. Andrews may, with a good explosion shot, get out and lie dead, but few can pitch over it so accurately that they can do so. A bunker similarly placed to the Road bunker may be made to accentuate this distinction. It may be constructed with so much slope that on occasions it may be possible to putt out of it.

I remember, shortly after the war, watching the contestants in the Open Championship or some other important competition playing the seventeenth at St. Andrews. One of the competitors had pulled his second shot wide of the road bunker. I said to the friend who was with me, "Here comes an American. Watch him pitch over the Road bunker and land in the road beyond." Instead of doing so, he played at

Clive Haswell

MacKenzie's famous "scabs".

68

a little hillock, only three feet across, to the right of the road bunker, and his ball curved in a complete semicircle and lay dead at the pin.

I said to my friend, "That is the best player I have ever seen. Let's follow him to the clubhouse and find out what his name is." We did follow him and we found his name was Walter Hagen.

Hummocks on the edge of greens are often constructed so that they assist the man who has opened up the hole correctly. They act as a hazard only to those who have failed to do so.

On many of the British Championship courses there are a succession of hillocks and hollows on the immediate approach to the greens. They extend, in many places, to within a yard or two of the place where the flag is usually situated.

These hillocks and hollows make it essential to play a running up approach to the greens. They create a most fascinating variety of approach shots which never bore and never tire the golfer. A golf course which merely caters for an everlasting pitch at every hole can never be entirely satisfactory. Any player under a sixteen handicap can play a pitch shot, but few of even the best players can play a run up shot. Bobby Jones never appreciated the Old Course at St. Andrews until he had learned to play this shot.

To see Joyce Wethered play the Old Course is an eye-opener. One hole she will play with a pitch with a terrific amount of backspin, another with a pitch with topspin and run, another with a scuffle along the ground as if it were played with a putter, and yet others with a curve from left to right or from right to left. I believe that she is the greatest player the world has ever known. She has not the power of many of the men players—in fact she appears frail and fragile—but she has a greater number of shots in her bag. I wrote an article some time ago expressing this view, and quite recently my attention was drawn to an article by Bobby Jones, who is undoubtedly the best man player who ever lived, expressing the same views. Just prior to the last Ama-

Walter Hagen, one of the few Americans who could play the Old Course the way it was intended to be played.

teur Championship at St. Andrews, Joyce Wethered played a four-ball match with Bobby, her brother and Dale Bourne. At the 15th hole, if I remember rightly, she was two up on any of them.

It is amazingly difficult to reproduce a course with the variety of approach shots so characteristic of St. Andrews. In the first place, construction is a very difficult art and can be carried out only by skilled superintendents under the supervision of the architect. In the second place, it requires exhaustive chemical tests of the soil to discover the most suitable fertilizers and seeds to produce the required turf. In the third place, it requires great care in mowing and upkeep to keep the turf up to a standard permitting shots of this kind.

Finally, the golfing public have not been educated up to it and, like Bobby Jones when he first visited St. Andrews, are only too prone to condemn it.

It has already been told how a new committee at Moortown altered some of the approaches of this kind on their course and how the members complained that they had taken all the interest and excitement away from these holes and demanded that they should be restored to their original condition. I do not know of a single course out of the more than four hundred we have done which has ever had any drastic changes to the original routing, or even the position of the greens.

In this respect we have always obtained finality, but I know of several where ignorant green committees have shaved down the undulations which created the charm and variety of the approach shots. Not only is this most unwise, but it is as much an affront to the architect as it would be to an artist to alter one of his paintings without his agreement. The cry of freakishness has only to be raised by prominent professional or amateur players who have not been educated up to playing any approach except with a pitch, to have the effect of persuading the green committee to flatten out these desirable features. On every occasion the course has become less interesting, but unfortunately, unlike the case of Moortown, the member rarely realizes why it has become so.

MacKenzie pitching to the 1st green at Alwoodley.

Sitwell Park, which has been illustrated in Robert Hunter's excellent book *The Links,* is a case in point. Before play commenced it was criticized by an ignorant press. Then the course became so popular that there was a big influx of members. Some years afterwards the course was played by prominent professionals and was again criticized. The committee thought that if players of world renown criticized it there must be something wrong, so they altered some of the greens. The result has been that the course has become so fair that it escapes criticism, but it is so dull and insipid that I have been informed that the membership has fallen from nearly six hundred to about half that figure.

The pee wee courses have come and gone. Like ships that pass in the night they have merely left their ripples behind. Ripples, incidentally, which have really done an appreciable amount of good. The pee wee course was too freakish to remain, but during its brief span of life it made many converts to golf and created a demand amongst golfers for an increased variety of approaching and putting on the courses already existing.

Although even the memory of the pee wee course is almost forgotten, some of the ideas have remained. The approach and putt courses, which embody much of the variety of the approaches and putting of some of the old natural courses with their sand dune country, have become more popular. Before this time I did not know of a single really good approach and putt course anywhere in the world. The reason, I think, was that golf clubs did not think it worthwhile calling in a first class architect to do such a small thing as an approach and putt course. Moreover, there are very few architects who are able to make an eighteen hole approach and putt course with an entirely different type of approach at every hole. They may have seen some of the old sand dune courses, but few have made a close study of them so that they have not the practical experience to make something really interesting.

I recently played over an approach and putt course in Los Angeles which was said to have been laid out by an architect who had written a book on golf, a statement which I can hardly believe. Almost every hole was a monotonous pitch on to a small green completely surrounded by bunkers. Can one imagine anything more dull and uninteresting? The good players would soon tire of playing the same shot time after time, while on the other hand the course was impossible for the average golfer.

As we played the first hole there were two people struggling to get out of the bunkers guarding the green, which was so small that every time they got out they rolled into the bunker on the other side. Eventually they waved us through. By the time we had played the ninth hole they were still ploughing their shots into the sand of the bunkers at the second. For all I know they are still trying to get on to the third green.

There is a similar approach and putt course at an indoor school in London, England. At first sight it looks a pleasing little course. There are presentable copies of the type of bunkers made by the best architects, but when one plays it disillusion comes. Every hole, except for a slight difference in length, is almost the same. Since I wrote this paragraph many of the bunkers have been converted into grassy hollows and the course has now become much more pleasurable and interesting.

As I have already said, on most golf courses there are far too many bunkers. A golf course should be made interesting and a good test of golf by the tilt of the greens and the character of the undulations. This principle is of special importance in the case of miniature courses. We recently made two eighteen hole courses for the Jockey Club at Buenos Aires. The ground was dead flat—in fact there was hardly a three foot rise on it—but fortunately at one end there was a twelve foot drop which enabled us to get drainage outside the property. We made all the ground extremely undulating by constructing a series of irregular swales radiating to the lowest point, and these swales gave us the following advantages: they cheapened and facilitated the drainage. They gave us plenty of soil for making greens and creating undulating ground, and above all, they gave the place such a natural appearance that the undulations appear to have been created by the effects of wind and water thousands of years ago. The course has a greater resemblance—not only in appearance but in the character of its golf—to the Old Course at St. Andrews than any inland course I know.

When we had completed the contouring of this course, which incidentally was done in twenty-one days, the captain of the club, a very able man and a student of golf architecture, asked me what I was going to do about the bunkering. I replied "The undulations have created such a varied, interesting, and pleasurable test of golf that we do not require a single bunker; nevertheless for the sake of appearance and for the purpose of creating more spectacular thrills we will give you a few bunkers."

The fascination and lasting interest of the game of golf would be vastly increased if one were always faced with an "approaching" problem.

It cannot be stated too frequently that a golf course which permits the best results to be attained with a pitch at every hole is certain to become monotonous. Variety is everything, or nearly everything, and if golf courses fail to give variety the game cannot continue to retain, let alone increase in, popularity. There is a great fascination in playing a shot with a maximum of topspin and seeing one's ball climbing over hillocks, through hollows, curving right to left, or left to right, and finally lying dead at the hole.

There is a feeling of suspense in wondering whether it is going to climb the last rise, followed by a feeling of intense relief when it just makes it and rolls down the final slope towards the hole.

Of course, one often puts topspin on a ball by topping it, and it is for this reason that shots with a deliberate topspin are not sufficiently appreciated except at St. Andrews, where many of the natives are adept at it.

It is interesting to hear the comments of the old cronies leaning on the railings overlooking the 18th green at St. Andrews which run on the following lines: "Mon wasna thaa-ata graund rinnin up shot of Charlie MacFarlane. That Sassenach (Englishman) he's playin' wi' is no gowfer, he tried to pitch it and cam back into the hollow." At St. Andrews one rarely hears a word of appreciation for a pitch shot, whatever the result may be, but a run approach usually gives rise to favourable comment.

There is nothing like the same excitement in watching the flight of a ball through the air. Then it is only the result which gives satisfaction. The manner in which a shot is played is a greater lasting pleasure.

At the risk of being boresome I have given a considerable amount of space to emphasizing the importance of creating variety in approach shots, as I feel that progress in golf architecture is dependant on creating courses of this description. There are a few other general principles which might be alluded to before I close this chapter.

There is, for example, the question of the length of the course, length of holes and details similar to these, but they are of minor importance compared with the main object of making the course interesting. Designers of golf courses have laid down the law as to the total length of the course, the exact number of one-shot, two-shot and three-shot holes and even the sequence of these holes in the round. How often have I seen a golf course ruined in the attempt to extend it to what is generally considered championship length.

Some of the committee who choose the courses for championships are responsible for this. They are obsessed with length and allow it to outweigh much more important considerations. It would be possible to make a golf course measuring 5,000 yards a much finer test of golf than some of those approaching 7,000 yards on which championships have been played.

The president of a club to which I belonged thirty years ago made the announcement that they were going to lengthen the course up to 7,000 yards and make it the best course in Britain. They succeeded in making it the worst. Some time afterwards it was remodeled and shortened by a thousand yards. It then became so popular that its membership nearly doubled.

It is true that there are certain general considerations which should influence us in routing a course. It is an advantage to start off with three or four long holes to get people away. It is also advisable to arrange the short holes so that they will be a rest after playing one or more of the long ones.

I usually like to have four one-shot holes, two in each half, but on occasions we have had as small a number as two or perhaps three, and on other occasions as many as five or six. We should be influenced primarily by the nature of the ground and what is going to give the best test of golf and the most lasting pleasure to the greatest number.

It has often been suggested that holes of a length which has been vulgarly described as "a drive and a spit" do not make good golf holes. There are many holes of this length which provide a more exciting test of golf and greater interest and subtlety than any holes I know. The 7th and 16th at St. Andrews and the 8th and 9th at Cypress Point are examples in point.

On most golf courses the three-shot holes are extremely dull, but on occasions, like the 14th hole at St. Andrews, they are most fascinating. Good three-shot holes should also be excellent two-shotters for very long hitters and, conversely, good two-shot holes should be interesting three-shotters for weaker players.

❦ Talking of two-shot holes, I recently ran across Tom Webster the cartoonist and Leo Deigel, who hailed me with the remark "Here comes old Two-Shotter." The allusion did not register and so I asked them to explain it. "Don't you remember" they said, "playing with us and Max Behr at Alwoodley? At the fourth hole you said to Max 'Here's an excellent two-shotter.' When you had both played half way you were in the rough on one side and Max on the other. You called out to him 'How many have you had Max?' He answered 'Six, how many are you?' 'Seven' was your reply." ❦

The 9th hole at Cypress Point, as an example of one of the best short par 4's in golf.

Jim Langley

This conversation took place when we were down at Sandwich, on which occasion Bobby Jones asked Tom Webster if he were playing for the St. Georges Vase. "No," said Tom, "I don't like vases."

It has often been suggested that an uninteresting hole might be improved by lengthening it, but it would be a safe axiom to adopt, "It will only be made worse and take longer to play. Shorten it and get it over."

It is generally acknowledged that a golf course should finish with three or four long holes. The advantage of this is that the player who is two or three down has still a chance of squaring or of winning his match, and it frequently results in the interest of the match being sustained right up to the end. This is a point, however, on which one must not be too dogmatic. The nature of the ground may not lend itself to four long holes. As an example, Cypress finishes with two one-shot holes and two drive-and-pitch holes, and yet I think it is the most exacting and terrifying finish of any course I know. At any rate I do not recall any course where one has a greater hope of winning or of squaring the match after being two or three down.

The last two matches I played there were cases in point. I was playing the best ball of two long hitters but dubs who gave me two up. Playing the 15th I was three up but one of my opponents got a two to my three, leaving me two up. At the 16th they both put their tee shots into the ocean whilst I played safe but was on the edge of the green. On my way towards the green I met my wife who was sketching and said to her, "I'm two up and both these blighters are in the ocean. I've got their five dollars in my pocket." However, one of them was not in the ocean—he was lying among rocks on the seashore. He played a miraculous shot up over the cliff and lay dead.

I fluffed my approach and lost the hole I seemed certain to win. At the 17th I topped my drive into the ocean and lost that hole, making us all square. At the 18th they were both on the green with their seconds—one of them two feet from the pin. I fluffed my drive and second, then played a spec-

MacKenzie on the eighteenth hole at Cypress Point.

tacular sliced third round the trees onto the green and holed my putt. I refused to accede the two-foot putt, he missed it, and so we squared the match.

We all had engagements in the afternoon but decided to desert our wives and families (they did not mind*) and play a return match. On this occasion the positions were reversed—they were three up and four to go. They had a series of disasters and we again squared the match.

Golf courses that provide thrills of this kind will not only be popular, but will increase in popularity. I rarely see an alteration to a golf course by a green committee that is a complete success.

When discussing the question of altering a hole, the chief consideration that should exercise the mind is "are we going to add appreciably to the interest and excitement of the hole?" Unless we are convinced of this we should leave it alone. My experience is that golf courses altered by green committees are almost always a failure. There are occasions when success has been achieved by a benevolent autocrat who has dominated a committee, but there must be no compromise—it must be a one-man show.

⊰ Trees ⊱

There are other debatable questions regarding general principles which occur to me, such as the value of tree hazards. There are many fine golfers who unhesitatingly condemn trees on a golf course, their argument being that there are no trees on an old sand dune course. This is so, but, on the other hand, on an inland course the only way, except at enormous expense of providing hazards as high as sand dunes, is by the use of trees in groups.

These critics also submit that there is too much of the element of luck in negotiating trees, but these same critics

---

*The parentheses were put in by my wife.

welcome whin bushes as hazards because they occur on sand dune courses, notwithstanding the fact that they often give rise to a still greater element of luck.

As I have stated before, there are more mistakes made in the designing of golf courses by attaching too much importance to the element of luck than anything else.

Most of the best inland courses owe their popularity to the grouping of trees. Groups of trees are the most effective way of preventing players reaching the green with their second shots after playing their drives in the wrong direction. No bunkers guarding the green seem to be able to prevent them doing so.

On how many occasions have I made a hole and said to myself, "We will guard this hole so heavily from the right- or left-hand side that no one will be able to stop his shots on the green unless he has placed his tee shot in the right position." Then up comes Cyril Tolley or Ted Ray and after the wildest of drives takes a mashie-niblick and lays his second dead at the pin. I remember Cyril Tolley playing the 6th at Cypress Point. The hole is nearly five hundred yards in length, and was designed so that if the player desires to reach the green in two shots it is essential for him to carry a bunker on the right about two hundred and twenty yards from the tee. Cyril Tolley pulled his tee shot and then found a group of high fir trees intervening between him and the hole. Instead of playing back onto the fairway to which he belonged, he attempted to carry these fir trees and eventually took seven or eight for the hole.

At first sight Tolley was inclined to condemn these trees, but I feel sure that he is such a good judge of golf and golf courses that if he played the hole more frequently he would realize that this group of trees gives him an enormous advantage over a weaker driver. Cyril Tolley was quite capable of carrying the bunker two hundred and twenty yards from the tee and then having a wide open shot for the hole. On the other hand, the ordinary player is forced to play to the left of the tee-shot bunker and is then faced with the difficult problem of skirting this group of trees and, even if he brings off the shot successfully, he is still a long way from the hole.

Trees should not usually be placed in a direct line with the hole, as they block the view too much. They make an excellent corner for a dog-leg. Firs, pines, cypress, silver birch and Californian oak make beautiful backgrounds for greens. All these evergreens are suitable for a golf course, while on the other hand, deciduous trees make a mess and look out of place.

Playing down fairways bordered by straight lines of trees is not only unartistic but makes tedious and uninteresting golf. Many green committees ruin one's handiwork by planting trees like rows of soldiers along the borders of the fairways. Alternatively, groups of trees, planted irregularly, create most fascinating golf, and give players many opportunities of showing their skill and judgment in slicing, pulling round, or attempting to loft over them. Some of the most spectacular shots I have ever seen have been around, over or through narrow gaps in trees.

A short time ago I constructed a second course for the St. Charles Country Club in Winnipeg. Their existing eighteen hole course was on flat, almost featureless country. The greens and bunkers are nothing out of the ordinary, but the trees have been cut down in a most artistic manner, leaving clumps scattered irregularly over the fairways. Without these trees the course would have been exceedingly dull and uninteresting, but as it is, it is one of the best courses in Canada. The most important of the principles in designing and constructing a golf course is to make the fullest use of trees and all other natural hazards and features.

I always attempt not only to make every hole different on a golf course, but never conspicuously to reproduce two exactly similar holes. I attempt to get inspirations by seizing on any natural features and accentuating the best golfing points on them. For instance, I observe a small hollow in the ground, or a small rise, perhaps not more than two feet in height, and accentuate this to possibly ten times the size.

In this way not only is variety obtained, but every artificial feature created harmonizes with the natural surroundings. If we discuss too many general principles we may be apt to lose sight of the main principle of making a course full of interest and excitement. One often finds one or more members of a committee obsessed with some pottering detail. One thinks that it is a sine qua non (essential) that the short holes should be equally divided among the odd and even numbers of the holes so that in a foursome—often in America termed a Scotch Foursome—each player has an opportunity of playing an equal number of tee shots. Others are disturbed at the possibility of danger arising from crossing rarely used roads, or the proximity of two adjoining fairways.

Danger! Ye gods, when one has given them a hundred and fifty yards in width, and on the Jubilee course at St. Andrews in places there is less than fifty yards for both fairways. These objections not infrequently come from some peppery old colonel who has faced shot and shell scores of times and yet is afraid of a golf ball.

Others are perturbed because one or two of the holes are played into the evening sun, and if a course runs east and west it is sometimes impossible to avoid this. Others think the tees are too near the greens. At St. Andrews every tee except the first is part of the previous green.

When I hear all these objections I often feel inclined to tell them the story about the lady and the rhinoceros. In case you do not know it I will tell it to you. If you do know it you can skip from here to the next chapter.

⋈ A lady scientist was interested in the sex of animals. She knew, for example, that the female spider was much fiercer than the male, and other interesting things of that sort. One day she visited the Zoological Gardens where there was a new rhinoceros and she asked the keeper what was its sex. He did not know but referred her to the foreman. The foreman, after considerable hesitation, admitted that he did not know but he was certain that the superintendent would. She went to see the superintendent, but he was out. Again she called, but he was still out. Finally she caught him about six o'clock in the evening. She told him her errand. He hemmed and hawed and after much beating about the bush was forced to confess that he did not know.

The good lady was terribly distressed, and after telling him she had been seeking him all day and was astonished that a man in his position did not know the sex of this rhinoceros, he replied "Well after all madam, what the hell does it matter except to another rhinoceros?" ✦

MacKenzie and Jones walking what would become Augusta National. "If, as I firmly believe, the Augusta National becomes the World's Wonder Inland Golf Course, this will be due to the original ideas that were contributed by Bob Jones."—Alister MacKenzie

❧3❧
Economy in Golf Course Construction

To obtain the best possible results at a minimum of cost is the guiding principle of golf course construction.

The more one sees of golf courses, the more one realizes the importance of doing construction work really well, so that it is likely to be of a permanent character. It is impossible to lay too much stress on the importance of "finality." Every golfer knows examples of courses which have been constructed and rearranged over and over again, and the fact that in every country millions of dollars are frittered away doing bad work which will ultimately have to be scrapped is particularly distressful to a true economist.

As an example of unnecessary labour and expense, I have in mind a green which has been entirely relaid on four different occasions. In the first instance it was of the ridge and furrow type. The turf was then lifted and it was made dead flat. A new secretary was appointed, and he made it a more pronounced ridge and furrow than ever. It was then relaid and made flat again, and has now been entirely reconstructed with undulations of a more natural outline and appearance.

In discussing the question of finality it is well to enquire if there are any really first class courses in existence which have been unaltered for a considerable number of years and still remain not only a good test of golf but a source of pleasure to all classes of players; to see if there is any golf course which not even the rubber cored ball has spoilt; and if so to find the cause of its abiding popularity.

The only one I know is the Old Course at St. Andrews, Scotland. It was the most popular course in the world in the days of the feather ball, the guttie and the Haskell, and today Bobby Jones considers that not only is it the best course in the world, but he says that he gets more joy in playing it than a hundred other courses. Today, with the exception of the lengthening of some of the tees, St. Andrews remains substantially the same as it was seventy years ago.

This, as well as some of the other British Championship courses to a lesser extent, still retains its popularity among all classes of amateurs. In fact, it is characteristic of all the best courses that they are just as pleasurable, possibly even more so, to the long handicap man as to the player of championship rank. This fact upsets the argument which is often used that the modern expert tries to spoil the pleasure of a player by making courses too difficult.

The successful negotiation of difficulties is a source of pleasure to all classes of players.

The origin of St. Andrews is shrouded in mystery, but the fact of the matter is that St. Andrews differs from other courses in that it has been deemed a heresy to interfere with its natural beauties and it has been left almost untouched for centuries. No greenkeeper has ever dared shave down its natural undulations, most of the bunkers have been left where nature placed them. Others have originated from the winds and rains enlarging divot marks left by players, and some of them possibly by the greenkeepers, converting those hollows where most players congregated into bunkers, owing to the difficulty of keeping them free from divot marks.

The bunkers at St. Andrews are thus placed in positions where players are most likely to go, in fact in the precise positions which the ordinary green committee would suggest should be filled up.

Hell bunker.

AGJ

This is a significant fact and tends to show that many of our existing ideas in regard to hazards have been erroneous. It has already been stated that Mr. John L. Low pointed out years ago that no hazard is unfair wherever it may be placed, and this particularly applies if the hazard is visible, as it should be obvious that if a player sees a hazard in front of him and promptly puts his ball in it he has chosen the wrong place.

⊁ I once heard a tale of a Yorkshire farmer finding a man in his coal house during a coal strike. He put his head through the window and said, "Now I've copped you picking out all the big lumps." A voice came back out of the darkness: "You're a liar. I'm taking them as they come." ⊁

On the old type of course like St. Andrews, the players have to take the hazards as they come, and do their best to avoid them. There is nothing new about the ideas of the so-called golf architect. He simply wishes to reproduce the old ideas as exemplified in the old natural courses like St. Andrews, those courses which were played on before overzealous green committees demolished the natural undulations of the fairways and greens and made them like lawns for croquet, tennis, or anything else except golf, and erected eyesores in the shape of straight lines of cop bunkers instead of emphasizing the natural curves of the links.

In the old view of golf there was no main thoroughfare to the hole; the player had to use his own judgment without the aid of guideposts or other advantageous means of finding his way. St. Andrews still retains the old tradition of golf. For example, I have frequently seen four individuals playing the long hole (the 14th), deliberately attacking it in four different ways, and three out of the four were probably right in playing it the way they selected.

At St. Andrews, "it needs a heid to play gowf," as the caddie said to the professor. St. Andrews is a living example of the possibility of obtaining finality.

There are many golf course architects whose courses have never been appreciably altered. As I mentioned in the last chapter, I do not suppose that Abercromby's or Harry Colt's courses have ever required material alterations, and I am quite certain that Max Behr's Lakeside course at Los Angeles and his other excellent courses will always remain as they are at present.

It often happens that a club employs an architect and, contrary to his advice, carries out the work themselves so as to avoid paying for his supervision. Neither the construction of a new course nor alteration to an old one can be a complete success by these methods.

Some years ago I advised the Prestwick Club, who owned a magnificent piece of links land and had one of the most famous of the British Championship courses, regarding new 7th, 8th, 9th, 10th, 11th, and 12th holes. The committee decided to carry out the work themselves. The general opinion of the club is that the changes have been a great improvement on the old holes, but I know, and doubtless other golf architects know, that they have made a complete mess of some marvellous natural golfing country.

I was particularly distressed regarding the 11th hole. I visualized it as becoming the most famous of all one-shot holes, whereas the design and construction has been so badly carried out that it is a very indifferent hole.

When a green committee carries out an architect's plans, the result is rarely even a partial success, and in any case the committee takes the credit for any improvement and the architect gets the blame for any failure. This is true to such an extent that bitter experience has taught us to refuse all work unless we are allowed a free hand in interpreting our own plans.

In the attempt to obtain finality it is of primary importance that the advice of the architect is taken in its entirety. Cases not infrequently arise when clubs have not sufficient money to carry out his plans completely. Then the work should be carried out as indicated in the first chapter, and improvements made from year to year as more funds become available.

Founders of golf clubs are often deterred from calling a first class architect because they think he may be expensive. An architect's fee is often less than a hundredth part of the total capital expenditure, and surely this is a small sum to pay for the assurance of perpetual prosperity.

I cannot recall a single example of the failure of a golf club that has taken the advice of a first class architect. Even men of education have a curious disinclination to pay for mental labour. They are willing to pay stupendous sums for manual labour, but for mental labour, No!

It is strange that a committee consisting of doctors, lawyers, architects, and engineers who no doubt recognize the importance of mental training and experience in their own professions attach so little importance to it in golf course architecture. What does it matter what the fee of the expert is if, owing to his advice, the total cost can be reduced fifty percent and far better results obtained in addition? It is false economy to attempt to save a few thousand dollars in mental labour when without it there would be an additional cost of tens of thousands of dollars in manual labour. The unfortunate thing about golf courses is that every professional and almost every golfer thinks he can lay out a golf course.

A short time ago I had a letter from a Scottish professional hinting that the time might come when I might be retiring, and suggesting that I might adopt him with a view to his carrying on my work. I replied to his letter inquiring about his education and asking him if he had made a study of psychology, if he had been educated at an agricultural college and had acquired a knowledge of chemistry, botany, geology and engineering, and above all had he any training and love for art?

I pointed out that though it was essential a golf course architect should have an intimate knowledge of the theory of the game of golf and make a close study of all the best courses, yet the ability to play the game was often harmful, as first class players only too frequently were subconsciously influenced by their own particular type of play and only too prone to disregard that of others.

I remarked before, that although I know scores of excellent golf courses designed by amateur golfers, I did not know of a single outstanding one by a professional golfer. Not that there are not plenty of professionals who are men of considerable education, but the fact that they are constantly playing competitive golf makes them view with resentment anything that is likely to disturb their sequence of threes and fours.

I have a great admiration for J. H. Taylor. Winner of five British Open Championships, he is one of Nature's gentlemen, is exceedingly well read, has original and common sense views on health, politics and many other subjects, and moreover is a born orator and writer. On the other hand he is not a success in designing golf courses. At one time, because he was unable to play it with a pitch, his favourite shot, he condemned the 17th at St. Andrews in most emphatic terms. Recently he admits that, having given up competitive golf, he has changed his views, and in picturesque language puts a curse on anyone who would dare to alter it.

I have selected J. H. Taylor as the representative of the professionals not only because of his marked ability, but because in England he is the spokesman of the Professional Golfers Association and for many years was their president, and may be so still as far as I know.

We have always told each other in the frankest manner possible our respective views, and one thing I admire more in J. H. Taylor than anything else is the fact that he is not afraid of changing his ideas and admitting he has changed them when one has given him a sufficiently logical reason to convince him that he is wrong. Many years ago, when Harry Colt and I were designing most of the golf courses in Britain, J. H. Taylor started an agitation to prevent us doing so, and tried to make golf course architecture a monopoly of professional golfers.

We contended that if it were not for the amateur golf course architect there would be very few professionals, and it was as a direct result of modern golf architecture that there had been such a boom in golf and golf courses. Subsequent events, I think, proved that we were right, and that the very existence of most of the professionals is due to the fact that golf architects have made inland courses popular. There would be very few professionals if golf were still confined to sand dune country by the seashore.

J. H. Taylor is a professional at Mid Surrey, a marvellous piece of sandy links in the heart of London. Some years ago the course was reconstructed at enormous expense. Owing to the influence of J. H. Taylor, the approach to every hole was converted into a pitch. The result is a remarkably fine golfing land ruined, and the erection of a dull monotonous course. If an architect like J. F. Abercromby or Harry Colt had altered it they would have got better results at a tenth of the cost. The most serious mistake made by a golf committee is the fallacy that they will save money by neglecting to obtain the best expert advice in regard to fresh construction work.

Except where the course has been designed and the construction work supervised by the modern golf architect, there is hardly a golf club of any size which has not frittered away hundreds of dollars in doing bad work all for the want of the best advice in the first instance. There can be little doubt that the poorer the club the more important it is for it not to waste its small funds in doing the wrong kind of work, but to get the best possible advice from its inception.

A well known club in forming a golf course stated that the committee had decided to lay it out themselves, as they were afraid of a golf architect making it too difficult for the average player. Now this is precisely what the modern golf course architect does not do. He in particular adopts a most sympathetic attitude to the beginner and long handicap player, but at the same time attempts to make the course interesting to all sorts and conditions of players. It is characteristic of the modern architect that he always leaves a broad and pleasurable road that leads to destruction, that is sixes and sevens on the card of the long handicap player but a straight and narrow path which leads to salvation in the form of threes and fours for the "scratch man." The new course I designed for Bob Jones, the Augusta National, is ideal in this respect. It provides shots which the greatest of all golfers has the utmost difficulty in carrying out successfully, and yet it has only twenty-two bunkers, no rough, and is a paradise for the average golfer.

I once stayed at a golf club situated in the most delightful sand dune country which I chose for my vacation in great part owing to the fact that I had seen the land before and had also seen Mr. Colt's plan for the construction of an eighteen hole course which should have been the finest in England. On arrival I found that the green committee had, through motives of false economy, refrained from getting Mr. Colt to supervise the work and had done it themselves. The outcome was an expenditure of three or four times as much as Mr. Colt would have needed, the destruction of many of the beautiful undulations and natural features which were the making of Mr. Colt's scheme, the conversion of magnificent visible greens into semi-blind ones, banked up like croquet lawns, and a complete absence of turf owing to wrong treatment, alterations in the placing of greens, tees, and bunkers, with a total disregard for the beginner and the long handicap player. On a British seaside course in particular, little construction work is necessary, but the important thing is to make the fullest use of existing features. Five thousand dollars in labour expended under expert supervision is better than a hundred thousand injudiciously expended.

Surely in the case of a golf club it is more important to have an architect for the course, and any new work on the course, than for the clubhouse. Much more costly mistakes are made in constructing the former than in building the latter.

One can readily imagine what would be the ultimate result of a course laid out by an average committee composed of scratch, three, four and eight handicap men. They are most of them, probably subconsciously, prejudiced against any hazard being constructed into which they are likely to get themselves. But they are all unanimous in thinking that the poor devil with a twenty-four handicap should be left out of consideration altogether. The final result is neither fish, flesh, fowl nor even good red herring.

The expert in golf architecture has to be intimately conversant with the theory of playing the game, but this has no connection with the physical side of playing it. An ideal golf expert should have not only a knowledge of botany, geology and particularly agricultural chemistry, but should also have what might be termed an artistic temperament and a vivid imagination.

We all know that there is nothing so fatal in playing golf as to have a vivid imagination, but this and a sufficient knowledge of psychology to enable one to determine what is likely to give the greatest pleasure to the greatest number, are eminently desirable in a golf architect. The training of the expert should be mental, not physical.

I have devoted a considerable amount of space to emphasizing the importance of expert advice in obtaining economy in golf course construction. Even in America there are many sites for golf courses on which, if they are properly designed, they require no manual labour, with the exception of that necessary for fertilizing, seeding and irrigation.

On links land of this description, our greatest difficulty is the *prevention* of manual labour. In this connection a skilled superintendent is of almost as great importance as the architect, who must know his job and be wide awake, for one of his workers with a scraper may destroy, in a few minutes, a small hummock which would be the making of the hole. Fortunately today there are many skilled superintendents available who have had many years experience of working under the best architects. Even these skilled men require continual reminding that they must leave natural features alone unless their destruction has been ordered by the architect.

Robert Hunter, in his book *The Links,* points out that some new holes were constructed at Deal after the war. He says, "There was such a marked contrast between them and the old holes where Nature had been left undisturbed that he resented playing them." These new holes were constructed by a professional at considerable cost and would have been vastly better if not a cent had been spent on them except for topsoiling, fertilizing and seeding. Robert Hunter, in the same excellent book, in emphasizing the economy in construction of getting the best advice, states, "My most earnest advice to members of any club undertaking to construct a course is this: If you seek something permanent, something that will give you real satisfaction and not be a heavy drag on your purse for many years, employ your architect only after the most careful inquiry and get the best man available regardless of his fees. There is a finality, that is the important thing, about the work of the best men which is worth tens of thousands to any club." The primary essential, therefore, in designing and constructing a course so as to obtain the best value at a low cost is to substitute the excessive cost of uncontrolled labour by machines controlled by experts.

In the first place, every precaution must be taken to route the course so as to make the best use of all natural features. In the second place, a skilled superintendent is required who is able to interpret the architect's plans and has sufficient experience to conserve all the best natural golfing features and to make any artificial ones as indistinguishable from the natural as is humanly possible.

One of the most important considerations is to instill into the mind of the manager of the construction company, the superintendent and all the men employed, the absolute necessity of never doing any manual labour if it can be done more cheaply by machinery. As an example of the kind of mentality required to get work done at the lowest possible cost, I may quote the Valley Club at Santa Barbara. When the course was constructed, apart from the irrigation system, for

$44,800, a large portion of the ground was rocky and had to be covered with soil.

The Managing Director of the American Golf Course Construction Company, Mr. Robert Hunter, introduced a new machine, a caterpillar tractor with a bulldozer attachment, to remove the large rocks and boulders. He thus saved thousands of dollars in explosives and manual labour. He also erected a loading device to save the excessive cost of loading carts by hand and by various other means saved large sums of money. We have known golf courses where similar difficulties were encountered but they cost four or five times as much as Santa Barbara.

When we first designed golf courses there were no golf course construction companies available, so we had to undertake all the work in conjunction with some local greenkeeper or landscape gardener. In addition to this we had to rely on our own puerile efforts in soil technology, drainage, irrigation and other engineering problems.

We had also to depend on the good faith of seeds merchants in regard to seed and fertilizers, as well as using our own ingenuity in devising or advising upon labour saving devices to decrease cost. As an instance of this, twenty-five years ago there was not a single scraper or scoop available in Britain. We resented the price of manual labour and made inquiries in regard to less costly methods for doing the construction work. A result of our inquiries was that we discovered the existence of scoops in Canada, so we arranged to have some of them sent to Britain and have used them ever since. At Moortown we were faced with the problem of turfing thirty acres of fairways. We devised a turf cutting machine which would cut an acre of sods in four hours. We also designed a mole drainage machine which enabled us to do the draining at less than a tenth of the cost of ordinary manual methods.

When we first constructed golf courses in America we worked out our own system of irrigation, but since then we have discovered far better and cheaper results are obtained by employing specialists in irrigation problems. At the same time it is only fair to say that our hoseless system was much superior to other systems in existence in many parts of America.

When Wendell Miller and I were at Pine Valley recently the greenkeeper there told us that at times they required as many as eighteen men to water the course. This, of course, is exceptional, as the average course requires only about six men.

At Pasatiempo, where an up-to-date completely hoseless system designed by a specialist in engineering was adopted, all the fairways are watered by one man. If necessary he waters as many as half the fairways in one night and the next night waters the other half. There are no hose pipes required on even the tees and greens, so it is not difficult to compute the difference in cost of upkeep by a hoseless system similar to that at Pasatiempo compared with the antiquated irrigation by hoses.

It is true that the initial capital expenditure of a hoseless system is greater, but the saving in cost of upkeep would probably pay this extra expenditure off in three or four years. There are other advantages of the hoseless system. If it is well designed, far less water is required, as it can be arranged so as to give most water to the plateaus that require it and less to the hollows. As the cost of water is often extremely heavy, this is a very great saving. Hoses, on the other hand, get worn out or stolen, and this, in addition to the extra cost of water and the cost of more manual labour, adds considerably to the cost of upkeep.

At one time I thought I knew a great deal about the drainage of golf courses, and perhaps twenty years ago I knew more than most people, but I have got more black marks over drainage than over anything else. Today I realize that drainage is a specialist engineer's job and that a club gets far better results and less costly work in employing a man who has devoted his whole time to it.

I have just been reading this to a friend, a friend not noted for his refinement. He smiled and I asked him, "Why this ribald laughter?" He said, "The word 'specialist' always

One of the more difficult one-shot holes to be found.

reminds me of the book by the same name, and particularly the last sketch depicting the carpenter specialist sitting in his battered old Ford car on the top of the hill every Sunday afternoon surrounded by an adoring family viewing with rapt admiration his latest masterpiece, the eight holer."

This is an age of specialists.

Experience has taught me that it is in the best interest of clubs that an architect should devote all his time and thought to the design, strategy and sculpturing of the course and put the problems of irrigation, drainage, and the details of designing labour saving devices and other problems of a similar nature to people who are better qualified than himself. Nevertheless, an architect should have enough knowledge of all these special subjects to be able to advise clubs as to how they can get the best and cheapest results.

Many committees raise the objection, "Why should we pay any fees except the architect?" "Why should we pay a contractor, a soil technologist, a botanist, a geologist, an irrigation or drainage engineer?" The answer to all this is because in this way you will get by far the best value at the lowest cost. You may be paying more for trained minds, but you are lessening your chief expense—manual labour. Why should a club worry about the cost of specialists if, owing to their advice, the total cost is half of what it would have been without them and the result is the last word in construction? As a general rule, the more a club pays for mental labour, the less the total cost will be.

One of the dangers of seeking advice from a builder of golf courses who offers to do the work for a small fee is that he may attempt to supplement his income by secret commissions from seedsmen and others. In cases of this kind the club members are only too frequently being robbed both in regard to price and quality of the goods. The International Society of Golf Course Architects prohibit their members receiving or giving commissions.

The only real safeguard a club has for getting a course constructed cheaply and well is the reputation of the architect. Cheap advices, or work on a contract basis, usually

Mac, his wife Hilda, and Marion Hollins on the 10th tee at Cypress Point. Note MacKenzie's DeSoto, below the 7th green.

leads to secret commissions and disaster. Designing golf courses is an art, and like other forms of art requires education, experience and a flair for the particular subject.

If it is desired to design a palatial mansion, public building or attractive hotel, it is usual to choose a first class architect who, after making the plans, advises on the best specialists in stone, brick, concrete, iron, woodwork, interior decorations, plumbing, furniture, landscape gardens and all the thousand and one things which go to make up a beautiful establishment. Similarly, in regard to golf courses, we find we obtain the best and cheapest results not only by ensuring that finality is obtained in the routing and designing of the courses, but also in advising our clients as to the best specialists in the construction and contour work, drainage and irrigation engineers, soil technologists and botanists to guide us in the choice of pure unadulterated seeds and so on.

At first sight it might appear that the fees of all those specialists might increase the cost of the work. In actual practice it is by no means that case because as I stated previously the excessive cost of manual labour is displaced by the comparatively low cost of mental labour.

The Cypress Point Course had perhaps within one year of its inception greens and fairways freer from weeds and clover than any course in the United States.

O. B. Keeler, the biographer of Bobby Jones, stated in the *American Golfer*, "Cypress Point and Pebble Beach are the finest golf courses in the world today. Cypress Point is a dream, spectacular and perfectly designed. The courses in California are so much better than those in the rest of the country that I have no basis of comparison." Whilst another great golfing man, Hans Samek, the President and father of the German Golf Association, stated in the *Canadian Golfer,* "Cypress Point is a fairy tale, an unbelievably beautiful course. Cypress Point and Pebble Beach stand out as the two finest golf courses I have seen in the world, including the famous seaside courses of Britain or the Continent and along the Atlantic Coast."

Cypress Point was made on the scientific principles I have outlined in the foregoing pages. It was not a question of luck or sowing a mixture of various seeds in the hope that one or more would suit the particular soil conditions, but real concentration of thought and principle. As an example of the time and thought involved in the work, Mr. Robert Hunter, who was then my Californian partner, after consultation with me, drew up ten pages of typewritten memoranda in regard to methods of carrying out the work. The following are some of the extracts.

Obtain reports from the following experts of the University of California:

Professor Shaw	A soil map of property.
Professor Kennedy	A study of grasses and weeds.
Professor Weir	A map for necessary drainage.
Professor Bard	Report on soils requiring nutrition and the treatment of soils under trees.

Lay out turf plots and test out following grasses:

German mixed bent	Triticum Repens
Yarrow	Cynosurus Cristatus
Poa Trivialis	Festuca Duriuscula
Blue grass	Agrostis Canina Capillaris
Red Top	Metropolitan Bent
Red Fescue	And native bents selected by
Sheeps Fescue	Kennedy.
Agrostis Maritima	

One plot of fine sand fertilized chemically
One of sand covered with an inch of clay
One of sand and loam harrowed in three inches
One of sand mixed with compost and loam poisoned with arsenate of lead.

Some of the soil tests received showed the following:

Analysis of soils at	5th green	18th green	4th fairway
pH	5.9	8.4	6.9
% Organic matter	5.2	9.5	6.9
Available phosphorus	Low	Very High	Low
Calcium carbonate, etc.	0	34.2	.005
Lbs. sulphur required to Give pH desired	250	100 tons	600

Note pH 7 is neutral. The desired acidity is pH 4.5.

The soil on the site of the 18th green was excessively alkaline owing to the presence of abalone shells. We riddled the soil so as to eliminate the larger shells and then contented ourselves with making the top inch acid.

Directly the grass was up we increased the acidity with frequent dressings of sulphate of ammonia. Before construction work commenced we discussed the advisability of steaming the soil to obtain a clean seed bed and we sent samples of all the seeds to three universities to check their purity and germination.

It is owing to scientific methods of this kind that in California we have succeeded in obtaining perfect greens and fairways free from weeds, daisies and clover. Before work commences we try to impress on the construction company the importance of highly paid and highly skilled men with a maximum of horses and machines. The kind of man we require is one who is continually using his wits in order to make the best use of the natural features and to construct artificial features indistinguishable from natural ones.

We try to avoid employing the type of man illustrated in the story about the English bishop and the railway employee.

✤ In Britain at every big railway station there is a man employed to walk about the trains and tap the wheels with a hammer to find out by the sound if the wheels are cracked. A bishop got into conversation with one of these men and elicited from him that he had worked for the railway company for thirty-five years and had never had a day off. The bishop said, "Splendid! What a good and faithful servant you are. If the country had more men like you what a magnificent country it would be to live in. Now tell me, what do you tap these wheels for?" The faithful employee scratched his head and said, "Blowed if I know!" ✤

In attempting to employ highly paid men we are frequently hampered by members of a committee—usually those members who in the first instance were opposed to employing a first class architect. They contend we are paying more than the usual union or district rates, and it is difficult to persuade them that we will get better and cheaper results by these means. At times they even insist on reducing the men's wages, and this is fatal, as they take no more interest in their work. You have lost their brains and only have the use of their hands. On the other hand it is a good plan to commence by giving low wages but to tell the men that as they become more skillful their wages will be increased.

A policy of this kind acts as a stimulus and the men are constantly striving to give better and greater service. In actual practice, experience has taught us that a few extra cents paid in men's wages is worth many dollars in actual production. Our experience of both British and American workmen is that they are very fine fellows and appreciate a word of encouragement and praise, but above all they appreciate being taken into one's confidence. There is nothing that makes them take such an interest in their work as explaining to them why you want the work done, in what at first sight appears to them to be an unusual kind of way.

The best workmen take a pride in doing what they have been taught is a good workman-like job. In other words, their natural tendency is to make everything neat and tidy in regular circles or in straight lines and angles and one of the most difficult things with which one has to contend is to break them of this ingrained habit and get them to follow the irregular curves of nature. It is only men of great intelligence who can be trained to do difficult work like the sculpturing of a golf course.

Similar principles apply in the construction of a golf course as in any other well-run business. The superintendents and men are encouraged to be continually devising new means to get the work done in the most economical manner.

A conscientious architect and construction company are even more particular in saving a club's money than they are their own. Experience is continually teaching us cheaper and better methods of doing construction work. It is needless to say that the contouring of greens, tees, hillocks, hollows, bunkers and so on can all be done with tractors and scrapers cheaper than hand labour or even horses and scrapers. We have recently found that small tree roots and rocks weighing up to a ton or more can be removed by the caterpillar tractor and bulldozer.

The use of explosives should be reduced to a minimum by covering up the larger roots and rocks with soil and seed. This is not only the cheapest method of disposing of the roots and rock but has the advantage of making undulating fairways resembling real links land. We have also found by experience that explosives smash up rocks into small fragments. After the course is soiled and seeded these sharp fragments work their way through to the surface, whereas a rounded rock never does.

At Aberdeen, Scotland we had similar difficulties with which to contend. We found that we could tell the size of a rock by the character of the sound when we tapped it with a hammer. If it were a small one we removed it, but if it were large, we covered it with topsoil and seeded it. By this means also we made delightfully undulating fairways.

Unfortunately all our hard thinking was wasted. The

authorities who took over the course thought they knew more about golf courses than we did. They considered that these fairways should be flat and not undulating, and then proceeded to flatten them out by exploding the rock and then covering the fragments. They have been troubled ever since by these broken fragments of hard rock working through the surface.

This foolishness was quite contrary to all the stories I heard in Aberdeen of their reputation for caution and thrift. Here are a sample of one or two of them.

There were two Aberdonians in a boat when a storm came up and blew their mast away. Then a mist came on and they did not see land for three days and three nights, by which time they had come to an end of their food and their water. They came to the conclusion that the only thing to be done was to pray, so Donald went up into the bow of the boat to pray. His prayer ran like this: "Oh Lorrrd, me and Sandy are verrrry sinfu' fellers and this has come to a judgment to us for our sins. But Oh Lorrd if you deliver us out of ourrr troubles we'll promise you Lorrrd, we'll promise you—." A voice from the stern breaks into his prayer "Tonald, Tonaldt dinna promise. Ah think ah see land."

Here are some more.

An Aberdeen farmer was offered a hundred pounds for some cattle, less ten percent discount. He did not know what ten percent discount meant, so being cautious said, "I will give the matter ma verra carrrefu' conseederation and will give you ma answer tomorrow." In the meantime he went to the village hotel and saw Maggie, a very pretty girl, behind the bar. "Maggie" he said, "If I was to offer you a hundred poonds, less ten percent discount, what would you take off?" "Everything except my earrings," said Maggie with alacrity. ❧

❧ A local laird had grown some very fine grapes and sent some of them to the Queen at Balmoral. He got a gracious letter thanking him, and thought his gardener would appreciate seeing it, so he showed it to him and asked him if he did not think it very gracious of the queen. The gardener turned the letter over and over in his hand and after some hesitation said, "Weel, ah dinna see anything aboot her returning the basket." ❧

❧ As an old gentleman was walking down the main street in Aberdeen a Salvation Army girl asked him if he would give a shilling to the Lord. He said, "How old are you ma bonnie wee lassie?" "I'm seventeen," she said. "Ah weel," he replied, "I am seventy and ah'll be seein' the Lord before you will so Ah'll gie it him masel'." ❧

It is a strange thing about Aberdeen and most of the northwest of Scotland that they have more fallacious ideas about golf courses than other countries where Nature has not been so kind as in Scotland. We were rather proud of our course in Aberdeen and thought we had given them the best inland course in Scotland. It was an amazingly difficult course to construct, as it consisted entirely of pine trees, rocks, bog and heather.

We also had bad luck with the construction work. We anticipated we should be able to cart all the trees away over frozen ground in winter, but for the first time for twenty years there was not frost and so we had to make expensive roads over the bogs. We saved a tremendous amount of labour and avoided the removal of tree roots and rocks by covering them with soil and utilizing them to make undulating ground like the marvellous links land they have in Aberdeenshire. It was particularly galling to find that our efforts were not appreciated.

It was not until afterwards that we discovered that

although all the golfing world flocks to Scotland, the Aberdonians themselves fail to appreciate their wonderful natural links land and use any money they obtain to destroy their natural beauties. It is indeed fortunate that they have not much money in Aberdeen or there would be no links land left there.

I have just been re-reading some of the articles I wrote over twenty years ago on economy in golf course architecture and find that even today, so applicable are they, that some of my remarks may be reiterated.

The cost of carrying earth can often be reduced to a minimum by using a little thought on the work. The stone from stone walls, rocks, the turf from turf walls, or soil taken out of excavations should never be carted away as they can always be utilized for raising a neighbouring green in the form of a plateau or in making hummocks or large undulations indistinguishable from the natural ones which are so delightful on seaside courses.

It is rarely necessary to cart soil from a distance for the purpose of making a hummock or a green. It is much more economical to remove a sufficient area of turf from, and around, the site of an intended hummock or green and utilize the soil so removed from around the hummock for this purpose.

This method has a double advantage. The surrounding ground is lowered as the hummock is raised, and makes the hummock appear higher, while at the same time it is made to merge imperceptibly into the surrounding hollow or hollows and gives it a far more natural appearance in consequence. A hollow removed from the front of a green has the effect of making the green appear as if it were raised upon a plateau, and this is still further accentuated if the soil removed is also used to build up the green.

It is essential, however, that these hollows in front of the greens should drain into larger hollows at the sides. The turf at the bottom of the hollows should be so dry that it permits of a run up shot.

On many courses we have done recently we have

mapped out the whole of the golfing area into a series of large swales all draining into the lowest part of the property. By these means we have not only lessened enormously the cost of the drainage but on flat land we have got plenty of soil to build up greens, make artificial hummocks and above all give the whole golf course such a natural appearance that it simulates real links land of wind and water formation.

The green and the bunkers guarding it should all be made at the same time. The soil moved in making the bunkers can then be utilized in the formation of the green.

It was, in former years, considered imprudent to construct bunkers until the experience of playing revealed the proper positions, but since those days our knowledge of greenkeeping had advanced. An expert can judge by the character of the grasses and the nature of the undulations the amount of run which the ball is likely to get, and this knowledge, combined with actual measurements, gives more information than it is possible to gain by playing. Perhaps the most important reason why the architect's scheme should be completed in the first instance is that bunkers are hardly ever placed in the right position afterwards.

As I have mentioned before, it is difficult to find a member who is not subconsciously prejudiced against constructing a bunker he is likely to get into himself.

In constructing bunkers, greens and other features on a golf course, carting is rarely necessary, and as it is often one of the most costly items it should be reduced to a minimum.

On the other hand there are occasions when a certain amount of carting is essential for transporting sand, fertilizers and topsoil on stony or sandy ground.

At Cypress Point we covered over thirty acres of sandy and sterile ground with three to six inches of soil. This would have been an enormous expense if we had loaded the carts by hand in the usual way, but we rigged up a loading device by means of an inclined plane. A scraper with its attendant pulleys was then attached by means of a rope to a tractor or horses. On reaching the top of the plane, the scraper was tilted and the soil tipped into the cart. By this means the majority of the costly manual labour was obviated.

Carting should, whenever possible, be done when the ground is hard in dry weather, or during frost, for if the ground is soft a considerable amount of labour is often necessary to obliterate tracks. Carts should not be allowed to wander about all over the place, but should be made to keep in one recognized track. It is often advisable to remove turf previous to carting, relaying it after the work is finished. Carts can sometimes be replaced with advantage by sledges with flat-bottomed runners.

Wendell Miller of the firm of Wendell Miller and Associates of Chicago and Columbus showed great foresight, energy and knowledge of labour saving devices when we constructed the Bayside Links at Bayside, Long Island.

On my arrival in New York, after previously submitting the plans, I found that Miller, in conjunction with the Bayside Golf Corporation who owned the land and were financing the project, had arranged most up-to-date machinery and economical devices for the construction of the course.

He had written hundreds of letters and sent scores of telegrams. In one week he had spent over two hundred dollars in telephone calls in his attempts to get the best and cheapest equipment in order to complete the construction work in a few weeks and have the course open for play within a few months.

When I arrived on the scene I found over thirty machines, including drag lines, sixty-horsepower caterpillar bulldozers, scrapers, drainage machines, stone removers, ploughs, disc harrows and others too numerous to mention. Any one of the five larger machines was capable of doing the work of two hundred men.

In five days when we got properly going we had nearly completed the drainage, pulled down over a mile of stone walls and converted them into hillocks, covering them with earth, completed the contouring of four greens with the surrounding hillocks, hollows and bunkers, and partially done eight more.

We had also started the machines for removing the stones from the fairway and had everything ready for the installation of a one- man hoseless system of irrigation of all fairways and greens. Miller had also made tests of several varieties of seeds and a chemical analysis of the soil of all the fairways and greens, and had arranged for professors from three universities to consult with us regarding the most suitable seeds and fertilizers to use on different parts of the property.

He had made tests of the most economical methods of moving earth by machines engaged on the job, and had drawn up a chart showing the length of haul for the most economical use of drag lines, sixty-horsepower bulldozers and the different scrapers and had arranged the work so that each one should be used in its proper place.

Strange to say two chairmen of green committees who were viewing the work made exactly the same remark to me, namely, "The use of these labour saving devices is the cause of unemployment."

"On the contrary," I replied, "the greatest contribution America has made to prosperity and the happiness of the world is that it has proved without a shadow of a doubt that wealth producing machinery not only causes high wages and cheap foods, but also employment. The reason for the present unemployment in the United States is due not to machinery, but to the fact that the stock exchange crisis created a loss of confidence in introducing new machinery and consequently everything came to a standstill. Consider this new Bayside course, for instance. If we had not shown by these new up-to-date machines that we could construct a golf course which was better than others, the Bayside Golf Corporation would never have agreed to the construction of a golf course at all, and everyone who is now engaged on the work would have been out of a job. As it is, the effect of the golf course in increasing employment will be very far-reaching. Men will be necessary for the upkeep of the course, engineers repairing and making new machines, increased employment for taxi men, shopkeepers, road builders, railway men and other inhabitants of Bayside. Moreover, the work is being done so well that the development company contemplates making two more courses, and this again will give still more employment and bring more people to Bayside to the benefit of everybody concerned."

It is an amazing thing to me that there are so many politicians and leaders of men in the world who have so little knowledge of economics that they believe efficient machinery and organization creates unemployment.

It should be obvious to any thinking schoolboy that if an industry fails to progress, everyone connected with it will soon be out of a job. It is a sine qua non that before anyone can be employed there must be a reasonable probability of obtaining a market for one's goods, and the best way of securing a market is to reduce the cost of production by wealth producing machinery. At Bayside we did things by means of labour saving machinery which we would never have dreamed of doing without it. Not only did we make outstanding greens, but we also constructed undulating fairways of a similar nature to St. Andrews and other Scottish seaside links.

Fourteen days after we commenced work, and notwithstanding six inches of rainfall and complete stoppage of work on several days, we completed the contouring of twelve greens and partially did five more, made hillocks of all the stones and stone walls, removed the tree roots and contoured some of the fairways.

A short distance from Bayside another golf course was being constructed, and it would be difficult to conceive of greater difference in the methods of construction. No architect and no experts had been engaged, but on the other hand I was informed that upwards of two hundred men had been employed for twelve months. These men appeared to have been engaged in leveling down the desirable features which we had been at such pains to create at Bayside. There does not seem to be a single hole of interest on the whole course. All the greens are alike, horseshoe shaped with a semi-circular bank. The fairways, at great expense, have been bordered by trees like regiments of soldiers. The trees are doing well, but on the other hand most of the grass seed failed to germinate. Would it be possible to conceive of a greater contrast between two methods of construction? One is completed in a few weeks, and the other after a year's work was still far from completion. The one had an architect, a construction company, four subcontractors, a superintendent, three foremen and six other experts, thirty machines and only ten labourers, the other has no architect and no expert except for irrigation, three machines and two hundred labourers.

On the one golf course undulating ground, which is characteristic of the best links, was made by machines. On the other these desirable features were being destroyed.

On one course every hole is different; on the other there is a sameness and a complete absence of strategy, variety and interest. One course is being constructed at an exceptionally low cost, while the other will cost more than twice as much, and when it is completed there will be no finality and no prospect of ever obtaining a popular course unless it is completely reconstructed. Which is the right method?

Every thinking man will agree that true economy can only be obtained with the aid of experts on the lines described in the construction of the Bayside Links, and yet in this enlightened age nine out of ten golf courses are being constructed with uncontrolled labour.

After the Bayside Links were opened for play, I was informed that during the worst of the Depression they took over ten thousand dollars every playing month in green fees, probably twice as much as other public courses in New York State.

The Augusta National has also been completed, and we profited by our mistakes and experience at Bayside. We all learn by the experience of mistakes, and have done an even better and more economical job than at Bayside. It is not long since the Augusta National has been opened, but its reputation is already worldwide.

Alister MacKenzie

❧4❧
Ideal Holes and Golf Courses

❧ *Why Players Give Up Golf* ❧

It is a remarkable thing about golf courses that nearly every man has an affection for the particular mud heap on which he plays. It is probably largely due to associations: his friends play there, he knows the course and can probably do a lower score than elsewhere. He may perhaps also have pleasant recollections of the dollars he has won from his opponents.

It may not be a real course at all. There may be no interest or strategy about it; it simply gives him an opportunity for exercise and "socking" a golf ball.

He is opposed to any alterations being made to it, but the time inevitably comes when he gets tired of golf, without knowing the reason why. Perhaps after spending a holiday on some good golf course he clamours for the reconstruction of his home course, or migrates elsewhere.

I have met at least three or four men at St. Andrews who

The first hole at Cypress Point—a wonderful start to a 2½ hour round of golf.

USGA

learned their golf at school or college and came to England. After playing there for a few years they gave up the game altogether. Not one of them realized that the reason the game had lost its charm was because they were no longer playing golf, but a very bad substitute for it.

We have known scores of clubs in Britain that have reluctantly called us in to reconstruct their courses, because they finally realized all their good players were leaving them for newer and better golf courses.

The West Herts Golf Club at Cassiobury Park and Tooting Bec Golf Club were cases in point. They were both losing members rapidly and finally had their courses completely reconstructed, thereby regaining their popularity.

Tooting Bec was in the heart of London. It was the old Parliamentary course where Arthur Balfour and all the leading golfers of the day were members, but the club lost them all and it was not until too late they realized the cause of the decline in membership. The club again became popular, but it has an entirely different class of member.

It is always a disheartening period for a club when it loses its most popular members, but this state of affairs could usually be prevented if committees made a point of visiting the best courses, enabling them to realize the defects of their own and take steps to have them remedied. I recently read an article in the *Fairway Magazine* by Joseph Blake. After stating that for years he had been completely satisfied with his home course, he goes on to say: "20 years of nationwide golf have just been schooling, educating me to the point when I could truly appreciate a masterpiece of golf course architecture when I saw it. The other day I teed off at number one hole at Cypress Point. Since then I've become a person with an 'idée fixe.' But I care not, for wedded and bound to the South, I have a mistress up North and I glory in her. She's wonderful! I shall often steal away and visit her. Never tiring, never criticizing, she shall be my adventure, and when I am done I shall return slow footed, my dreams touched by smiles, to my home down by the border."

A golf course architect perhaps is not the best man to

judge what is an ideal course. I myself am in all probability subconsciously prejudiced in favor of golf courses I have designed myself. I remember, while I was doing the plan of the Old Course at St. Andrews, sitting in the main room discussing different golf courses with some of the members. There was an old man sitting in his usual seat by the fire who was rarely known to speak a word. He was generally known as the "Stout King," and after drinking his fourteenth bottle of stout, interposed the remark, "I know the best course in the world." We said, "What is it?" He said, "Fan Ling." We then asked him who made it, to which he replied, "I did!" and not another word could we get out of him. We have since discovered that Fan Ling is a course in China and it has the reputation of being one of the best in the Orient.

There are few problems more difficult to solve than the problem of what actually constitutes an ideal links or an ideal hole, but it is comparatively safe to say that the ideal hole is one that affords the greatest pleasure to the greatest number, gives the fullest advantage for accurate play, stimulates players to improve their game, and which never becomes monotonous.

The real practical test is its popularity, but this brings us up against another difficulty. Does the average player really know what he likes himself? One often hears the same player expressing totally divergent opinions about the same hole. When he plays it successfully, it is everything that is good, and when he is unsuccessful it is everything that is bad. It frequently happens that the best holes give rise to the most bitter controversy. It is largely a question of the spirit in which the problem is approached, depending upon the player. Whether he looks upon it from the "card and pencil" point of view and condemns anything that disturbs his steady series of threes and fours, or whether he approaches it in the "spirit of adventure" of the true sportsman. There are well-known players who invariably condemn any hole for which they have taken over six, and if by any chance they ever reach double figures, words fail them to describe in adequate language what they think of that particular hole.

It does not by any means follow that when a player condemns a hole in particularly vigorous language he really dislikes it. It may be a source of pleasure to his subconscious mind, and whilst condemning it, he may be longing to play it again so as to conquer its difficulties. Who is the best judge of what constitutes an ideal hole? Is it one of our leading players, or any golfer who simply looks upon it from his own point of view? I have known of an Open champion expressing his opinion that a certain course was superior to any in Britain. As far as this particular course was concerned, it was generally admitted by amateurs that although the turf and natural advantages were excellent, it had not a single hole of any real merit. The local committee were also of opinion that it was monotonous and lacking in real interest, and had decided to have it entirely remodeled, before this world renowned Open champion persuaded them to change their minds by expressing such strong views in its favour. After the committee turned down the writer's recommendations for reconstructing it, the club lost many of its members. Ten years afterwards it was reconstructed by Harry Colt on similar lines to the previous recommendations and has since regained its former popularity.

There are, unfortunately, many leading players who wish a course to be designed so that it will favour their own play and will not even punish their indifferent shots, but will put any one below their particular standard out of the running altogether.

❧ *The Line of Charm* ❧

There are many leading players who condemn the strategic aspect of golf. They only see one line to the hole, and that is usually the direct one. They cannot see why they should, as in dog-legged holes, be ever compelled to play to one or the other side of the direct line. A bunker in the direct line at the distance of their long drives is invariably condemned by them, because they do not realize that the correct line is to

121

one or the other side of it. It is only fair that even an Open champion should occasionally have a shot that the long handicap man is frequently compelled to play. If a bunker is placed at the distance of a short driver, he is faced with the problem of whether he should play short, to the left or right, or make a special effort to get over it. Why should not a long driver be faced with similar problems?

I am often asked by committees why I have got so many dog-legged holes in my courses, and my reply is, "Because almost every good hole in golf is dog-legged for certain classes of players."

Analyze the holes on the Old Course at St. Andrews. There is hardly a hole where the correct line is direct from tee to green. We have pointed out before that Max Behr says the direct line is the line of instinct and if we wish to make a hole interesting we must break up that line and create the line of charm. It is true that in the best dog-legged holes, the longer a player drives, the more direct his route, but nevertheless there is usually a considerable risk with its accompanying thrill in going the straightest line to the hole. Dog-legged holes require judgment and headwork. The short and straight player can often overcome a longer driver by greater skill.

⚔ Horace Hutchinson, two-time British Amateur Champion, tells a story about a long hitting young friend of his who was playing in the British Amateur Championship. He was drawn against a dour old Scotsman who could drive barely half his distance but who was as cunning as a cage full of monkeys. Horace Hutchinson walked two or three holes with them and did not see them again till the 16th, when he was surprised to see his young friend, who he thought was a sportsman, sitting on a hillock smoking a cigarette while the Scotsman and both caddies were looking for a ball. H. H. said, "How are you getting on?" He said, "I'm two down." H. H. said, "Well you've got him at this hole anyway." "No," he replied, "It's *my* ball the old cock is looking for." ⚓

Then the question arises as to whether a course or hole be ideal from a medal or match playing point of view. If it is necessary to draw any distinction between the two, there can be little doubt that match play should always have prior claim. Nine out of ten games on most good courses are played in matches and not for medals. The true test of a hole, then, is its value in match play. The majority of golfers are agreed, I think, that an ideal hole should be a difficult one. It is true there are some who would have it difficult for every one except themselves, but these, who usually belong to the pot-hunting fraternity, may be left out of consideration. It is the successful negotiation of difficulties, or what appears to be such, which gives rise to pleasurable excitement and makes a hole interesting.

❈ *To Be Or Not To Be* ❈

Certain kinds of difficulties, however, should be eliminated. Into this class we can, I think, put long grass, narrow fairways, and small greens, because of the annoyance and irritation caused by searching for lost balls, the disturbance of the harmony and continuity of the game, the consequent loss of freedom of swing, and the production of bad players.

We can also eliminate blind greens, blind bunkers, and blind approaches. The greater the experience I have of designing golf courses, the more certain I am that blindness of all kinds should be avoided. The only form of blindness that should ever be permitted is the full shot up to a green whose position is accurately located by surrounding sandhills. Even in a hole of this kind, it is not the blindness that is interesting, but the visibility of the surrounding sandhills. At Royal St. George's in Sandwich, which we redesigned, it was not the blindness of the green, but the grandeur and impressiveness of the huge sand dune, that made the "Maiden" such a great hole.

J.E. Laidlay in the face of the Maiden bunker.

The difficulties that make a hole really interesting are usually those in which a great advantage can be gained in successfully accomplishing heroic carries over hazards of an impressive appearance, or in taking great risks to place a shot so as to gain a big advantage for the next. Successfully carrying or skirting a bunker of an alarming or impressive appearance is always a source of satisfaction to the golfer, and yet it is hazards of this description which so often give rise to criticism by the unsuccessful player. At first sight he looks upon it as grossly unfair that, of two shots within a few inches of each other, the one should be hopelessly buried in a bunker and the other should be in an ideal position.

If, however, he will give it further consideration, he will realize that, as in dog-legged holes, this is the chief characteristic of all good holes.

Holes of this description not only cater for great judgment, but also great skill. A man who has such confidence that he can place his ball within a few feet of his objective gains a big advantage over a faint-hearted opponent who dare not take similar risks. On a course with holes of this kind, match play becomes of intense interest.

In a perfect hole the surface, not only of the green, but the approach to it, should be visible. It is difficult, or even impossible, to judge an approach accurately unless the ground on which the ball pitches can be seen, besides which it gives great pleasure (or sometimes pain) to see the result of one's shot. In an ideal hole, the turf should be as perfect as possible and the approaches should have the same consistency as the greens, but it is by no means advisable to avoid entirely bad lies or irregular stances. There is not only much skill required, but an improvement of one's game results in occasionally having to play out of a cupped lie, or from an uneven stance. There are few things more monotonous than always playing from a dead flat fairway.

In an ideal long hole, there should not only be a big advantage from negotiating successfully a long carry for the tee shot, but the longer the drive, the greater should be the advantage. A shorter driver should also, by extreme accuracy, be able to gain an advantage over a long hitting but less accurate opponent.

An ideal hole should provide an infinite variety of shots according to the varying positions of the tee, the situation of the flag, the direction and strength of the wind, etc. It should also at times give full advantage for the voluntary pull or slice, one of the most finished shots in golf, and one that few champions are able to carry out with any great degree of accuracy.

But the great test should be that as players of all handicaps play golf, a hole should, as far as possible, be ideal for both scratch and long handicap players.

There are many famous holes, such as the Cardinal at Prestwick, which are by no means ideal, as in an ideal hole

Tom Doak

The 11th at St. Andrews—one of the ideal holes in the world.

there should always be an alternative route open to the weaker player.

⊰ *The 11th at St. Andrews* ⊱

I think the eleventh (the short hole coming in at St. Andrews) may be considered one of the ideal holes of the world. Under certain conditions it is extremely difficult for even the best player that ever breathed, especially if he is attempting to get a two, but at the same time an inferior player may get a four if he plays his own game exceptionally well. It has been suggested that the mere fact that it is possible to putt the whole length is an objection to it. No doubt the timid golfer can play the hole in this way, but he will lose strokes by avoiding risks. Even if an expert putter holes out in four strokes once in three times, he can consider himself lucky, and I do not know of a single example of a player achieving success in an important match by this means. If a cross bunker were constructed at this hole, it would become appreciably diminished in interest in consequence. The narrow entrance and the subtle slopes have all the advantages of a cross bunker without making it impossible for the long handicap man. The truth of these contentions has been borne out by attempts which have been made to copy and improve on the hole by a cross bunker.

There is no hole that has been copied more frequently than the eleventh at St. Andrews, but I do not know any copy that has the charm, the interest, or the thrills of the original.

This is largely owing to the fact that the subtle slopes of the green and approach are overlooked, and there are few, if any, architects who have the courage to give the same marked tilt to the green, being much too afraid of hostile criticism. An architect fears the cry of freakishness, and the uproar of the press, if, perchance, some popular competitor like Bobby Jones putts a little too strongly and his ball rushes down the steep slope into Strath bunker, which is not an infrequent occurrence at this hole.

Some years ago a friend of mine was playing in the Amateur Championship, winning his way into the third round. At the 11th hole, he put his tee shot into Strath bunker on the right, whilst his opponent was in the Hill bunker on the left. There was a large crowd following a pair, I think it was Blackwell and Hilton, who were playing the 7th, which crosses the 11th at this point, and the gallery deserted Blackwell and Hilton to see the fun. My friend and his opponent played out of these bunkers into the Eden beyond the green, and back down the steep slopes into the bunkers again, and after taking 14 strokes, were exactly where they started, but their positions were now reversed, as my friend was in the Hill bunker and his opponent in Strath. They finally halved the hole in 17, amidst huge cheers from the crowd.

✯ *Criticism* ✯

If an architect designs a hole that gives rise to incidents of this description he has not a hope of escaping hostile criticism. "Freakish," "Unfair" and "Not golf" are some of the mildest expressions used. Many of the unsuccessful competitors pour into the ears of a sympathetic press (many of whom have remained in the clubhouse and have not even seen the course) heart-rending accounts of their woes and the disasters that overcame them at these particular holes.

It is the architect (like the woman) who always pays. Holes that give rise to similar tragedies cannot be said to be inimical to golf. At St. Andrews there are many holes at which similar disasters may occur, and most of the conversation in the club, the hotels, and among the pressmen gathered there are concerning similar episodes.

Golf is a game, and talk and discussion is all to the interests of the game. Anything that keeps the game alive and prevents us being bored with it is an advantage. Anything that makes us think about it, talk about it, and dream about it is all to the good and prevents the game becoming dead.

At the same time it may be contended that some of these things are most unfair, but it depends on what we base the charge of unfairness. A relative of mine who did not know golf and had never played it, said, on hearing charges of unfairness leveled at a certain course, "In golf, do not all the competitors play to the same holes? Is it not the same for everyone? How then can it be considered unfair? I can understand in a game of tennis if one competitor was playing into the sun all the time and there was no changing of courts this might be unfair, but in golf if everyone is playing to the same holes under the same conditions how can it be unfair?"

In one of the earlier chapters of this book I stated I had always been accustomed to having my best work described as unfair, and that at first I was much disturbed because no one had described Cypress Point as unfair. On further consideration I came to the conclusion that the amazing beauty of Cypress Point disarmed criticism. When I wrote this the Californian State Championship had not been played at Pebble Beach and Cypress Point, and there is a very different tale to tell now. Some of the Southern California papers, whose remarks were probably inspired by unsuccessful competitors, complained bitterly that the architect of Cypress Point, desiring to make the course more difficult than Pebble Beach, had placed the pins in most unfair positions.

As a matter of fact, the architect was not even present when the positions for the holes were chosen. The same committee who placed the pins at Pebble Beach were entirely responsible for their placing at Cypress Point.

If a golf course, or the placing of the holes on it, had the effect of creating such an extreme amount of luck that the inferior player was able to compete successfully against a better class of player, it might be considered unfair, but during the championship at Cypress Point the exact opposite was the case, and an analysis of the scores showed that the better players had an advantage of fully three strokes more than they were entitled to according to their handicaps. I can

The Redan hole at North Berwick, one of the best and most copied holes ever built.

hardly imagine an ideal short hole which is not sometimes considered unfair by the unsuccessful competitor. Even Bobby Jones, who for perhaps the only time in his golfing career picked up his ball at the 11th hole at St. Andrews, was inclined to condemn it as unfair. Today, however, his greater knowledge and experience of the course have convinced him that it is the best of all golf courses.

The 11th hole at St. Andrews requires a greater variety of shots under different conditions of wind and changes in position of the flag than any other short hole. It also provides more interest, excitement, and thrills than any other hole, and for these reasons I consider it the greatest of all short holes.

Many people consider a complete island short hole a good one, but holes of this type can never be considered completely satisfying, as only one shot is required, namely, the monotonous pitch.

❊ *The Redan* ❊

The Redan at North Berwick is another fine hole which has been copied almost as often as the Eden at St. Andrews. The original hole can hardly be considered perfect, as it is too blind and there are too many bunkers which have no meaning, but the ideas embodied in the hole are excellent, and these ideas give an architect great opportunities of making interesting holes.

The Redan is 200 yards long, the master bunker covers the left half of the green, and there is a marked upward tilt of both the approach and the green from left to right, so that a player has the alternative of playing over the bunker or attempting a shot with a swing from right to left.

Keeping the general conception of the hole in mind, we frequently construct holes that may be played with a swing from right to left, left to right, or even from either side according to the position of the hole in the green.

Gibraltar at Moortown. Bernard Darwin speaks of it as a hole "of alarming excellence." It is a severe test for the scratch player but an easy four for the less ambitious.

⚔ *The Gibraltar* ⚔

Robert Hunter cites the Gibraltar hole at Moortown as one of the best of the "Redan types" of hole. When this hole was constructed, however, I had not seen the Redan, and, I regret to say, had never even heard of it.

The green of the Gibraltar hole has been constructed on a slight slope. The soil has been removed from the lower portion of the slope to make the bunkers and to bank up the green. The natural slope has been retained at the entrance to the green, like the eleventh at St. Andrews, and it is these subtle slopes, which lead a ball which has not been correctly hit into the adjacent bunkers, that have very much the same effect as a cross bunker without the hardship to the long handicap player.

The hole also shares with the eleventh at St. Andrews the necessity for an infinite variety of shots according to varying conditions of wind, position of flag, etc. One day it is a comparatively easy pitch with a mashie, normally it is a straight iron shot, sometimes a full shot with a trace of pull is required, and at other times it is necessary to slice so that one's ball is held up against the slope of the hill.

The green itself is delightfully picturesque and is extremely visible against a background of fir trees—in fact, it stands up and looks at you.

The contrast between the vivid green of the grass, the dark green of the firs, the whiteness of the sand, the richness of the heather, and a vivid background of rhododendrons, combined with the natural appearance and extreme boldness of the contours, gives one a picture probably unsurpassed by any other artificial hole.

It is not only a delightful hole to see, which at any rate appeals subconsciously even to the dullest of minds, but it is equally delightful to play and is less difficult than it appears. You feel you are taking your life in your hands, and it therefore appeals, as Mr. Bernard Darwin says, to the "spirit of adventure"—yet a well-played shot always gets its

MacKenzie, his wife Hilda, and Marion Hollins at the 16th tee at Cypress Point.

due reward. It is considered by many the best one-shot hole in England and the members get more pleasure and a greater thrill out of it than any other hole on the course. It is the favorite topic of conversation in the clubhouse, and it is the one hole above all others that remains in the memory of visitors, yet, strange to say, during the last 24 years we have had the greatest difficulty in preventing it being reconstructed.

Now that I am a resident in America and my restraining influence so far removed, I should not be surprised if it were altered. Some of the committee, backed by leading professional players, although admitting it is the best hole on the course, suggest that if the unfair tilt of the green was flattened out it would become still better. It wouldn't—it would become as flat as ditch water and just as uninspiring.

⚔ *The 16th at Cypress Point* ⚔

There is one exceptionally fine one-shot hole, namely, the 16th at Cypress Point, California, which so far no one has suggested should be altered. This hole, however, is of an entirely different character to that about which I have just written. Its excellence is not due to the tilt of the green, but to the amazingly beautiful and spectacular ocean hazard intervening between the tee and the green. To give honor where it is due, I must say that, except for minor details in construction, I was in no way responsible for the hole. It was largely due to the vision of Miss Marion Hollins (the founder of Cypress Point). It was suggested to her by the late Seth Raynor that it was a pity the carry over the ocean was too long to enable a hole to be designed on this particular site. Miss Hollins said she did not think it was an impossible carry. She then teed up a ball and drove to the middle of the site for the suggested green. The photograph on page 52 gives a good idea of the character of the hole. There are three alternative routes, namely, the direct route

135

The 15th green at Cypress Point. The large gallery is watching Miss Glenna Collett playing round the course.

over 200 yards of ocean to the green, an intermediate route over about 100 yards of ocean, and a still shorter route to the left.

A well-played shot to the lone Cypress tree with a nicely calculated slice gets the help of the slope and runs very near the green, enabling the player to run up a slight swale and still have a good chance of a three.

I doubted if this hole could be considered ideal, because I feared that, compared with the other Cypress Point holes, there was not a sufficiently easy route for the weaker player. My mind was set at rest a few months ago.

✽ I was traveling from San Francisco to New York with a man who is affectionately known as Billy Humphrey. He said, "What sort of a hole do you think your 16th at Cypress Point is? I don't think a hole is a golf hole that can be played with a putter." "On the contrary," I said, "I don't think an ideal hole is ideal unless it can be played with a putter, but we won't argue about that. What is your trouble?" He said, "Well, I was playing this hole against Herbert Fleischaker for two hundred dollars. [Herbert Fleischaker has the reputation of not being able to get a ball off the ground, but he is full of brains, is a very good approacher and putter, and often outwits a more powerful opponent.] It was my honour, and I put two shots in the ocean. Then old Herbert gets his putter, takes four putts to reach the green, wins the hole and two hundred dollars." I am afraid I was not unduly sympathetic. ✮

✽ *The 15th at Cypress Point* ✮

The 15th hole at Cypress Point is another short hole of an entirely different character. It has probably been illustrated in golfing papers more frequently than any hole that has been constructed in recent years.

It is not by any means ideal, as there are not a sufficient

The 8th at St. Andrews. "It appears absurdly simple, but so far from familiarity breeding contempt, it has precisely the opposite effect."

Tom Doak

number of alternative shots necessary to play it. It is at its best when the flag is placed on the little tongue of green that projects between the bunkers on the right. In this position one has the alternative of playing an extremely difficult pitch with the chance of a two, or playing safe to the centre of the green and being content with a three. The hole owes its reputation almost entirely to the beauty of the green and its surroundings.

❧ *The 8th at St. Andrews* ☙

A hole that at one time I despised was the 8th at St. Andrews. It is a huge flat green and is guarded by one small solitary bunker. It appears absurdly simple, but so far from familiarity breeding contempt, it has precisely the opposite effect. On medal days the flag is usually placed behind the bunker and it is surprisingly difficult to get near it.

A pitch over the bunker usually lands yards behind the hole. On the other hand, there is a ridge 100 yards from the tee on the right which runs diagonally towards the bunker. A well-played run up shot will climb this ridge, curl round the edge of the bunker and lie dead at the hole, but unless the ball has sufficient topspin to climb this ridge it will turn off at right angles and be deeply buried in the bunker to the left.

❧ *The 16th at St. Andrews* ☙

In describing ideal holes it is extremely difficult to get away from the Old Course at St. Andrews. I was much enamored of the strategy of the course when I wrote some articles on ideal holes nearly 20 years ago, but today I am still more amazed at its subtlety. Twenty years ago I described the 16th at St. Andrews as an ideal hole. Its idealism was largely in my own head and in reality its strategy is far more subtle than I

The 16th at St. Andrews. As fine a strategic and subtle hole as exists.

pictured it. I described it as follows: "The sixteenth (corner of the Dyke) hole at St. Andrews is almost ideal for its length (338 yards). It was a particularly good hole at the time of the guttie ball, and is so today for a short driver, like the writer. As in the majority of good holes, it is the subtlety of the slopes that makes it so. The green is tilted up slightly from right to left, and it would be a better hole still if the inclination were greater. It is also guarded by Grant's and the Wig bunkers on the left-hand side, so that the approach from the right is easy, as all the slopes assist the players, and the approach from the left is exceedingly difficult. The point about the hole is that it is so difficult to get into the best position to approach the green, because of the proximity of the Principal's Nose bunker to the railway, and the difficulty of placing one's tee shot in such a small space with all the slopes leading to the bunker. On the other hand, there is a perfectly easy route free from all risk to the left of the Principal's Nose, but the player in all probability will lose a stroke by taking it."

This description of the 16th was entirely wrong.

Herbert Fowler fell into the same trap and suggested the Deacon Syme bunker should be moved 10 yards to the left, so as to give a little more latitude to the long driver who plays between the Principal's Nose and the railway.

Some years ago I told Ted Blackwell I agreed with Herbert Fowler and thought the hole could be improved in this way. Ted Blackwell replied, "Then you would move it to the spot which I think is ideal for placing my drive."

Ted Blackwell is a man of action, but of few words, and gave me no reason why he attempted to place his drive on this particular spot. I watched him play the hole on several occasions afterwards and noticed that when he placed his drive on this particular place, he played a run up approach so near the flag that he not infrequently got a three. I then discovered that he took advantage of a small valley (which I had previously overlooked) in the bank of the green leading up to the place where the hole is usually cut on medal days.

If the tee shot is placed ten yards to the left or ten to the right, the advantage of this valley is lost.

Is there any course in the world that presents such subtle strategic problems? There are thousands of golfers who have played St. Andrews for years and have failed to solve them or even to see them. Ted Blackwell has played St. Andrews fifty years and it may have been thirty years before experience taught him how to play this particular hole.

In 1930 St. Andrews was at its best. The links were hard and dry, and at many holes it was impossible to pitch and stay near the pin. Not only was the run up shot essential, but it was necessary to play for position and attack the subtle slopes from the correct angles. When St. Andrews is at its best, it is always attacked most viciously, and I never heard it criticized more vehemently than during this particular year.

❧ *Comparisons are Odious, and Yet — !* ❧

A friend of mine on the Walker Cup Team (not Bobby Jones, for he perhaps is the most ardent of all the admirers of St. Andrews) said, "You surely cannot compare St. Andrews with Cypress Point?" I replied, "I agree, St. Andrews cannot be compared with Cypress Point. St. Andrews is first class, there is no second, and Cypress Point comes a very bad third."

The old stalwarts of St. Andrews were perfectly indifferent to these criticisms. They knew that most of the critics had never seen or played on a real golf course before so they could not be expected to appreciate its virtues.

The indifference of some of the old devotees of St. Andrews reminds me of an incident that occurred to me in a train many years ago.

❧ I was in a railway carriage traveling down the Ayrshire coast. The carriage was full of workmen when a dude with a monocle and a bag full of golf clubs got in. He sat down behind his newspaper. A friendly little workman opposite him tapped him on the knee and said, "You'll be gaein to Troon ah'm thinking?" The dude replied "No," and put up his newspaper. A few minutes elapsed and again the workman tapped him on the knee and said, "You'll be goin' to Prestwick I'me thinking?" He again replied "No," but much more vehemently. Another period elapsed and the friendly workman again tapped him on his knee. This time he put down his paper very viciously and glared through his monocle and was greeted with the remark, "Do you think I care a dom where you are gaein?" ❧

If the members of the Royal and Ancient cared a damn what the critics thought, all these fascinating undulations would have been shaved down and the world would have been deprived of the only golf course on real links land that has not been defaced by the hand of man.

There is probably not a quarter of the bunker area at St. Andrews that there is on other well-known courses; the course is made by its undulations. Even after years of study of the course, I am always discovering fresh and better methods of playing the holes.

❧ *The 10th at St. Andrews* ❧

At one time I thought the 10th hole was weak. It is of poor length (310 yards), there is no bunker of any meaning, and a width of over 100 yards to drive into.

Nevertheless, to have a good chance of a three, not only the second but the first shot as well must be placed with the greatest accuracy. In front of the green is a high bank sloping down towards and beyond the usual position of the pin on medal days.

A pitch shot played from the position of a straight drive is stopped by the bank or runs far beyond the hole. On the right of this bank, however, there is a V-shaped valley running

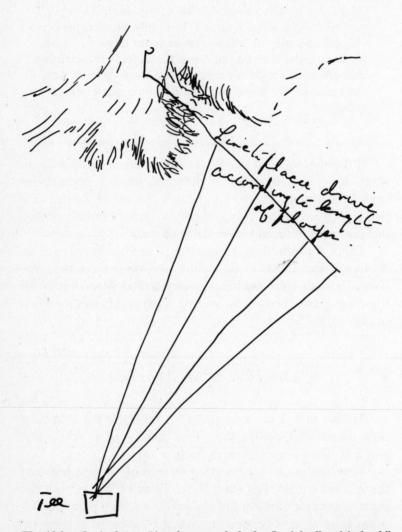

The 10th at St. Andrews. "Another great hole that I originally misjudged."

The 4th, "Ginger Beer," at St. Andrews. Joyce Wethered made more threes here than anyone else.

AGJ

towards the hole, so that if the drive is placed opposite this valley it enables a player to run up his second shot near the pin.

❧ *The 4th at St. Andrews* ❧

The fourth hole is another case in point. The green is guarded by a small abrupt hillock about 15 feet across. I always thought the correct way to play the tee shot was to the right, but Joyce Wethered pointed out that from this position you can only reach the centre of the green. She always plays it short of the cottage bunker to the left and from there plays her second against the left-hand side of the hillock and swings round very near the hole. I have never seen any one else play the hole in this way, but I am convinced Joyce Wethered gets a three there more frequently than any living person.

❧ *The 14th* ❧

Another hole which has several alternative routes is the 14th at St. Andrews. Some years ago I described it as probably the best hole of its length in existence. Here, again, the hole is made by the slope of the green. There is a most marked tilt up from left to right, so much so that it is impossible to approach near the hole from the right.

It is slopes of this kind that are so often overlooked in designing a golf course, and it is one of the most difficult things imaginable to construct them really well; but it is subtleties of this nature which make all the difference between a good course and a bad one. At the fourteenth hole at St. Andrews this tilt of the green has a considerable influence on the tee shot 530 yards away. Some years ago there were four of us playing four ball matches nearly every day for a month. We, according to our judgment, attempted to play this hole

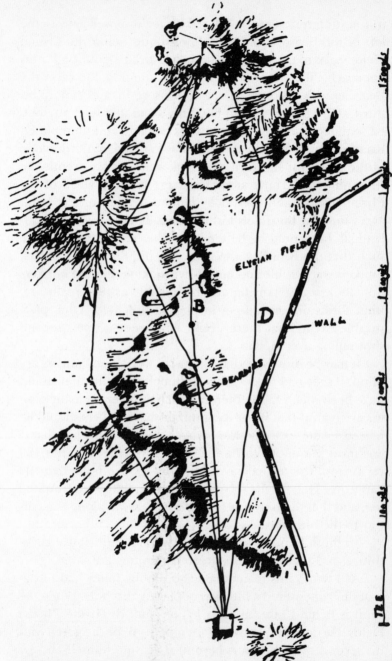

The 14th hole at St. Andrews. A,B,C,D are strategic lines to play the hole.

in four different ways. "A" played his tee shot well away to the left of the Beardies onto the low ground below the Elysian Fields, so as to place his second in a favorable position for his approach. "B", who was a long driver, attempted to carry the Beardies with his drive, Hell with his second, and run up his third. "C", who was a short but fairly accurate hitter, attempted to pinch the Beardies as near as he dare, and then played his second well away to the left, so as to play against the slope of the green for his third. "D" took what was apparently the straightforward route along the large broad plateau of the Elysian Fields, and eventually landed in Hell or Perdition every time; he invariably lost the hole. This hole is very nearly ideal, but would be better still if the lie of the land were such that the Beardies, the Crescent, the Kitchen, and Hell bunkers were visible and impressive looking. If these bunkers only looked as terrifying and formidable as they really are, what thrills one would get in playing this hole! What pleasurable excitement there would be in seeing one's second shot sailing over Hell!

It may be, however, that it is just as well these bunkers are blind. If they had been visible, although in reality they would have been much fairer, there would have been so many players crying out that it was most unfair that bunkers should be placed in the exact position where perfect shots go; that it was most iniquitous to have a hazard like the Beardies 180 yards from the tee exactly in the line for the hole; that the carry over Hell for the second shot is over 400 yards from the tee; and that the only way to play the hole was along the fairway to the fifth, etc., etc.

As these bunkers are blind, players do not notice these things, and the lives of the green committee are saved.

As I wrote this many years ago, Bobby Jones had not at that time discovered a fifth way of playing this hole. When the wind is behind him he plays his tee shot down the Elysian Fields. He does not, however, attempt to go for the green with his second shot, but plays beyond it, leaving himself an easy run up shot against the slope to lie dead and get his four.

⚔ *And The 17th* ⚔

The seventeenth hole at St. Andrews is almost too well-known to need description; it is probably the most noted hole in the world. Although so difficult, it is by no means impossible for the long handicap player, for he can go pottering along, steering wide of all hazards, and losing strokes because he refuses to take any risks.

At this hole, once more, it is the slopes that give so much character to the hole.

Even for the tee shot there is a ridge immediately beyond the corner of the station-master's garden which kicks your ball away from the hole if you pitch to the left of it, and towards the hole if you pitch to the right—in fact, an extra yard or two over the corner makes all the difference in getting into a favourable position for the second shot. There are also hillocks and ridges down the right-hand side, all forcing an inaccurately placed shot into an unfavourable position for the approach.

I often think that the hole would be more interesting without the Scholar's bunker; this prevents a badly hit second getting into the danger zone. If it were not there, one would much more frequently be forced to play the sporting approach to the green with the Road bunker intervening. It is this Road bunker, with the slopes leading a ball to it, which makes this hole of such intense interest. Notwithstanding the abuse showered on it, this bunker has done more to sustain the popularity of St. Andrews than any feature on the course. During the Open Championship some years ago, it was a joy to watch Bobby Jones play this hole.

On the three occasions I saw him play it, he avoided the mistake of playing it as a two-shot hole, but placed his second in a small hollow below the bank on the right of the green. A tablecloth would have covered the positions of the three balls. He then had an easy run up shot against the slope, laying his ball dead and getting his four. During the last 30 years there have been many good courses constructed in Britain

149

The 17th at St. Andrews. The most noted hole in the world.

and the United States, but to my mind none of them provide holes with such interesting strategic problems as these natural holes at St. Andrews.

The other British Championship courses consist of real links land, but many of them in their early stages were badly routed, and designed by golfers whose chief aim appeared to be to eliminate their natural sporting characteristics.

Two of the Scottish Championship courses, Prestwick and Troon, are excellent. Muirfield is not so good but has been vastly improved since Harry Colt reconstructed it.

⚹ *The 4th at Prestwick* ⚹

Many of the holes on the clubhouse side of the wall at Prestwick are full of interest and excitement. The fourth hole also, although it has not the bold features of many of the other holes, is an exceptionally fine dog-legged hole which owes its excellence to the curve of the Pow Burn.

This hole, incidentally, had the distinction of being condemned in no uncertain terms by a British Open Champion who also condemned the 17th at St. Andrews.

Troon is a delightfully situated golf course, and, unlike so many seaside courses, the view of the sea is not blotted out by sand dunes. During the last few years Troon has had over eighty additional penal bunkers constructed, of which number only one has added appreciably to the interest of the course. It was a much more pleasurable course to play and a much better test of golf before they were put in. The qualifying rounds of the Championship have on two occasions been played on the Portland course at Troon. The first occasion being two years after its construction.

The Portland course is further inland and has not the natural advantage of the sea or the magnificent sand dunes of the Old Course, but many consider it a better test of golf and more interesting. Unfortunately it is not kept in the same excellent condition as the Old Course, there is no water laid on the greens, and the club devotes most of their labour to old Troon.

⚔ *Gleneagles* ⚔

There are no outstanding inland courses in Scotland. Gleneagles enjoys a great reputation and is perhaps the most advertised course in the world.

I was the first golf course architect called in there, and saw it when there was scarcely a house within miles. I told them that at a cost of 3000 pounds they could construct the best inland course in Britain. It required hardly any construction work; the features were there naturally, the soil was light and sandy, it had irregular groups of magnificent pines and patches of gorse, and heather, and there was the most glorious view of the surrounding hills and mountains imaginable.

It is more or less common knowledge that over 50,000 pounds has been spent on the course, and of this sum a great deal was clearly expended in destroying the natural features which would have created its strategy and interest.

As it is the King's Course, although most spectacular and beautiful—it could hardly fail to be so among such marvelous surroundings—it is almost devoid of strategy, interest, excitement and thrills. There is hardly a hole where any strategical advantage is to be gained by attempting to place one's tee shot. It is sufficient merely to "sock a long ball" anywhere on the fairway, as the second is no easier, wherever the tee shot is placed.

There are many greens also which are visible from the tee and become less so afterwards. In other words, the actual surface of the green is invisible for the second shot, wherever one's ball is placed from the tee, and consequently, the holes at Gleneagles are by no means ideal. For they do not stimulate players to improve their games and they become monotonous. There are none of the little banks and hollows that make the British seaside links so fascinating. Players are most enthusiastic when they first play the course, but the more they do so the more their interest wanes.

Now St. Andrews is exactly the opposite: disappointment and even antagonism is followed (as in the case of Bobby Jones) by ever-increasing interest.

At Gleneagles there are no heated discussions as to the unfairness of the holes, because there is nothing to discuss.

⊰ Golf courses should be like the doctor who bought a practice in a country village. He put up his plate and waited for patients to come. He waited quite a long time, and as no one came he thought he would mix with the inhabitants a bit more. So each evening he would go down to the village pub and drink his tankard of beer with the old cronies. This, of course, was not strictly ethical and one evening one of the old habitees of the pub said to him, "Do ye know doctor, folk be talking aboot thee?" "Are they," said the doctor, "that's fine." "Aye, but ee doont know what they be a-sayin'," rejoined the yokel. "And I don't care a Tinker's curse what they be a-sayin'," said the doctor. "As long as they are talking about me, I'm satisfied." ⊱

There must be interest, and if there is no discussion, there can be no interest. Players lose their interest in golf without knowing why they have lost it. They grow stale.

At St. Andrews they may go off their game, but they never grow stale. There are no problems at Gleneagles; every hole is perfectly straightforward.

It may be said that the best golfers do not like problems. Golfers do, but mere sockers of a golf ball do not.

The point is, are we to make golf courses, like Gleneagles, which will never be criticized by the former class of players, or are we to make golf courses which will not only appeal to the latter but also to the average member of a club who is usually a man of education and a sportsman?

153

Unless we provide golf courses full of intricate problems, players will get sick of the game without knowing why they have got sick of it, and golf will die from lack of abiding and increasing interest.

There have been too many cooks at Gleneagles. Some of the work looks like that of an engineer and not an artist. On the other hand, there are some excellent holes on the Queen's Course, which, I surmise, have been designed by Major C. K. Hutchinson. It is a pity that all the work was not left to one man.

I understand there has been some talk of holding the British Championship at Gleneagles. It would be an evil day for golf if the Championship Committee ever departed from the principle of holding the Championship on real links land among the sand dunes by the sea. On the other hand, Gleneagles is a most delightful place at which to stay. It is perhaps the most beautiful and spectacular place of its kind in the world, and there is no air like that of the Highlands. The hotel is the best in Britain, and the gardens and grounds are, I think, the most artistic in Scotland.

In England, on the other hand, there are some excellent inland courses so good that they compare favourably with the English seaside courses. Woking and Sunningdale have already been mentioned.

❧ Lobb's Hole ❧

Worplesdon was the first effort of J. F. Abercromby, and has some excellent holes. One of them, I think the 15th, is known as Lobb's Hole. One of the principle characters in Sir James Barrie's play *Dear Brutus* was Lobb. The creator of the part was Arthur Hatherton, who was a very keen golfer and a member of Worplesdon. When Lobb was on his death bed he sent for his friend, Sir Gerald Du Maurier, and asked him if he would do him a favour.

Du Maurier asked him what it was.

He said "I want to be buried next to the 15th green at Worplesdon." Du Maurier said, "My dear fellow, you can't possibly be buried on a golf course." He replied, "No, but there is a corner of Brookwood Cemetery that runs up to the edge of the 15th green and I want to be buried there. The 15th green was always the turning point of my matches. These blighters always holed a long putt against me. I could not stop them when I was alive but I am going to do so when I am dead." So at the edge of this green there is a small statue of Lobb with his hands stretched out—"Thou shalt not hole that putt!" And the curious psychological effect of this is that today his old friends invariably miss their putts at this hole.

❧ Around the British Courses ❧

The Surrey and Berkshire outskirts of London are admirably adapted for golf courses. The best of them are among gorse, heather and pine woods. Immediately adjoining Worplesdon are Woking and West Hill, which have some excellent holes.

One of the best holes at Woking is the short 7th, where the designers have had the courage to put a bunker right in the middle of the green, and which is the making of the hole.

In the Sunningdale district are the new course at Sunningdale, Swinley Forest, Wentworth (three courses), Camberley Heath, and the Royal Berkshire Courses. The new course at Sunningdale is somewhat hilly but the short holes are excellent. Swinley Forest is a fine course, but as no competitions are held there and the club membership is strictly limited, it is not so well known as some of the others.

South of London are Addington, Coombe Hill, Walton Heath, and still further south, Liphook and Crowborough Beacon. The north of London largely consists of clay soil, so the natural conditions are not so favourable for golf. Moor Park, Hadley Wood, the West Herts Golf Club at Cassiobury Park are all good golf courses.

In the north of England, by far the best courses are in Yorkshire, notwithstanding the fact that with the exception of a small area around Doncaster and Ganton, Yorkshire consists of rock and clay. Alwoodley, Moortown and Ganton are all excellent courses. In the south of England, the best inland courses are those around Bournemouth and Eastbourne.

In the Midlands there are some good courses around Birmingham. There are hardly any outstanding inland courses on the east or west coast of England.

The real links lands among the sand dunes in Britain are perhaps as good as in Scotland, but compared with many places inland the most has not been made of these natural advantages. The majority would have been better if not a cent had been spent on construction work, and all the natural features had been retained as nature made them.

❈ *Hoylake* ❈

Perhaps the course that has been least disturbed by the hand of man is Hoylake.

Hoylake shares with St. Andrews the characteristic of at first sight being most disappointing. It looks flat and uninteresting, there are no trees, or even whin bushes and heather as at St. Andrews, and the surroundings are ugly. Nevertheless, the course is full of interesting, strategic problems, and the more one plays on it the more it is appreciated.

During recent years Harry Colt has eliminated the weak holes and constructed some excellent ones to take their place. Shortly after he had completed the alterations I visited Hoylake for the Open Championship. On entering the clubhouse I met one of the most famous of the English professional players.

He immediately attacked me as if I had been one of the authors of his misfortunes and said, "What do you think of the new 17th hole? I think it's the worst and most unfair hole I ever played." I told him I had not seen the hole so could not express an opinion, but when he left I turned to my friend and said, "I know his mentality. If he says it is the worst hole, I would not be surprised to find it one of the best on the course." And so it was.

"X" at that time was playing even better golf than Walter Hagen, who won, but he allowed this hole to get on his nerves and ruin his game. The attitude of Walter Hagen, who I think has the best temperament for golf of any living man, was an entirely different one. His argument was, "If the hole is difficult for me, it is equally so for the other competitors, so I must just make up my mind to conquer its difficulties." Which he did.

The 17th at Hoylake has somewhat similar strategic problems to the 17th at St. Andrews. It is also right up against a road and is tilted so that it has to be attacked at the correct angle, or else one is almost certain to slide down the slippery decline into the road.

If the tee shot is not placed in the correct position to the right, then it is desirable to refrain from playing for the green, and to play for the approach and take one's chance of running up dead and getting a four.

But this is only one of the good holes at Hoylake. The first is an excellent commencement to a round, and it also makes a good 19th. It is a marked dog-legged hole with an out of bounds on the right. It looks perfectly straightforward, free from hazards, but it is remarkable how many disasters occur at this hole. Its excellence is made by the angle of the dog-leg and the tilt of the green and the approach.

❧ *MacKenzie Greens* ❧

I was one of the first architects who refrained from flattening natural undulations of a green and who made artificial ones indistinguishable from nature. The consequence is that every freak green in Britain is termed a "MacKenzie Green."

During the championship at Hoylake, I was returning to

Liverpool by train in a railway carriage with a number of golfers who were discussing Hoylake and other greens.

None of them knew who I was, and one of them turned to me and said, "We have some of these infernal MacKenzie greens on our course." I remarked, "Was Dr. MacKenzie responsible for them?" He replied, "Well, they are called 'MacKenzie Greens,' so he must have made them." I asked him what was the name of his course, and he mentioned a course near Liverpool. Much to the amusement of the other occupants of the carriage, I remarked, "I happen to be Dr. MacKenzie. I have never seen or even heard of your blasted course, so how I can be responsible for your greens I don't know."

❈ Imitation is the Sincerest Form of Flattery, But—! ❈

One of the trials of a golf architect is that clubs attempt to copy his work, make an awful hash of it, and then blame the architect, who has never even seen the course.

Bitter experience has also taught me never to give advice unless definitely called in. The work is usually carried out badly and the architect gets the blame.

Within a short distance of Hoylake is Formby, an entirely different type of seaside course. It is secluded, very beautiful and appeals very strongly to golfers when they first play on it, but becomes somewhat boring afterwards.

It is marvellous golfing country, but the holes have been badly designed and constructed. There are none of the interesting strategic problems of Hoylake.

Farther north on the same coast is Lytham and St. Annes. Nearly 20 years ago I was asked to advise on the course. The turf of the fairways and greens at that time was probably superior to any British seaside course. The committee thought they had a second St. Andrews, but I am afraid I roused their ire by stating that they had not a single

The 140-yard short hole at Sitwell Park. A fiercely criticized green that has become universally popular and started the phrase "MacKenzie greens."

hole of any real merit. Since then the whole course has been reconstructed, and today it is so good that the worst hole is better than the best one existing twenty years ago.

In the southeast corner of England the links land on which the Deal and Sandwich Courses are situated is perhaps the finest in Britain. The courses, however, have not been so well routed, designed, and constructed as St. Andrews, Hoylake or Lytham and St. Anne's. On land of this kind it would be impossible to have uninteresting golf courses, but the most has not been made of the natural features, and at many holes some of the features have been completely destroyed. At Deal the holes near the clubhouse are fascinating, but the new ones further away, although difficult, are dull.

As we have stated before, Robert Hunter, the famous American golf architect, says it is always with a feeling of resentment that he plays these holes.

Princes is very long and difficult. The one-shot holes, although far from easy, have not the charm one has a right to expect on such magnificent golfing ground. There are some good dog-legged holes, but too many of a similar type—that is, a drive over a line of sand hills running diagonally away from the players.

The Royal St. George's Courses at Sandwich has more variety and, although not so difficult, has a more lasting appeal than Princes.

Further north, on the east coast of England, are Brancaster, Hunstanton, and Felixstowe; and on the south coast, Rye, Westward Ho, Saunton, and Littlestone, all situated on real links land.

⚜ *Saunton* ⚜

Tom Simpson has compared Saunton with the Old Course at St. Andrews, and has even gone so far as to say that today he thinks it the best of all courses.

It is magnificent sand dune country, even superior to its

better known neighbor, Westward Ho. Nevertheless, although more spectacular, it does not compare in interest, subtlety and thrills with the Old Course at St. Andrews. It has, however, the distinction of having been criticized in no uncertain terms by the majority of the American Women's Golf Team. Their captain, Marion Hollins, was an exception, but she knows and has played on real sand dune courses so frequently that she has learned to appreciate their virtues.

There are other courses in England situated among the sand dunes, such as Burnham, Harlech, Silloth, and Seascale, and many of these have some excellent holes.

⨯ Australia and Other Countries ⨯

There is some magnificent sand dune country in Adelaide and Sydney, and the golf courses in the neighborhood of Melbourne are reminiscent of Sunningdale.

Golf in New Zealand, unlike Australia, is dead. In fact, it has never been alive. Green committees there do not seem to realize that the game is played for pleasure; they utilize long grass as a penal hazard, and the consequence is that golfers will not put up with the annoyance of losing balls.

While in New Zealand, I designed a golf course at Maungakiki, Auckland (Titirangi). The construction of the holes appeared to be good, judging from the photographs they sent me.

They have a course in Rotorua, in the middle of the volcanic region, where the turf is as good as on any golf course. Its excellence seems to indicate that an excess of sulphur is favourable to the development of the finest of the dwarf golfing grasses.

The founder of the club was a cockney, and in addressing the preliminary meeting, said, "We will 'ave the only course in the world that 'as 'ot 'oles, for 'azards." The course is indeed full of 'ot 'oles where balls frizzle up and explode. At

161

intervals there are geysers spouting 100 feet or more, natives cooking and doing their washing in the adjoining hot springs, sulphur fumes everywhere, and many places where a stick is charred if it is pushed through the turf.

In South America there are some excellent courses. Mar De Plata is an excellent seaside course, and the Jockey Club, which has the reputation of being the richest club in the world, has recently constructed two first class inland courses which have complete hoseless irrigation systems. The land was originally dull, flat, and featureless, but it now has wave after wave of undulations and has a greater resemblance to the Old Course at St. Andrews than any inland course with which I am acquainted. If the upkeep of the course is anything like as good as its construction, it should become one of the world's greatest golf courses.

North America is rapidly becoming a greater golf center even than the home of golf, Scotland. The average American golf course is vastly superior to the average Scottish golf course, but I still think the best courses in Scotland, such as the Old Course at St. Andrews, are superior to any in the world. In the East, the National and Pine Valley are outstanding, and the excellence of many other courses may be traced to their shining example. My personal preference is for the National. Although not so spectacular as Pine Valley, it has a greater resemblance to real links land than any course in the East.

It is also essentially a strategic course; every hole sets a problem. At the National there are excellent copies of classic holes, but I think the holes, like the 14th and 17th, which C. B. Macdonald has evolved, so to speak, out of his own head, are superior to any of them.

❧ *Pine Valley* ❧

Pine Valley is, with the possible exception of Cypress Point, by far the most spectacular course in the world. I have never seen a course where the artificial bunkers have such a beautiful and natural appearance, and the undulations on the greens are excellent. On the other hand, I do not consider any course ideal unless it is pleasurable for every conceivable class of golfer.

Walter Travis was the best player of his day, and he was perhaps the most finished player that ever lived, yet I understand he was quite incapable of playing Pine Valley. He could not break a hundred.

There are many stories told of Pine Valley. One of them was about a man who habitually went round his home course in under 90. His friends bet him he could not break 150 at Pine Valley. He got as far as the 5th hole, where he put several shots in the lake. He then tried putting across the bridge but failed so often that he used up his 150 shots before he reached the 5th green.

Pine Valley is a striking example of where it would be so easy to give alternative routes which the weaker player might take for the loss of a stroke or proportion of a stroke, and at the same time make the course even more difficult and interesting for the good player. On some of the holes, such as the 18th, there are times when it is necessary for even the best player to play short, uninteresting golf shots when facing a strong wind.

The committee know our views, but they invariably reply, "We don't want any golfers at Pine Valley except those bordering on scratch." The time will inevitably come when the existing members will become older, and as they do so their length of drive will decrease, and why should they then be debarred from enjoying the course?

The Lido has some first class holes. One of them, the 18th, was made from my plan of a two-shot hole which won the first prize given by C. B. Macdonald in a competition in golf architecture. The design of this hole is reproduced in this book on page 166. Another excellent course on Long Island is Timber Point, on which the nine holes bordering the sea are particularly good.

Enormous sums of money have been spent on golf courses in Chicago. Some of them are good, but few outstanding.

Karl Olson

The 17th at National Golf Links. C.B. Macdonald's masterpiece.

The 5th at Pine Valley. Even some of the best players struggle on this hole.

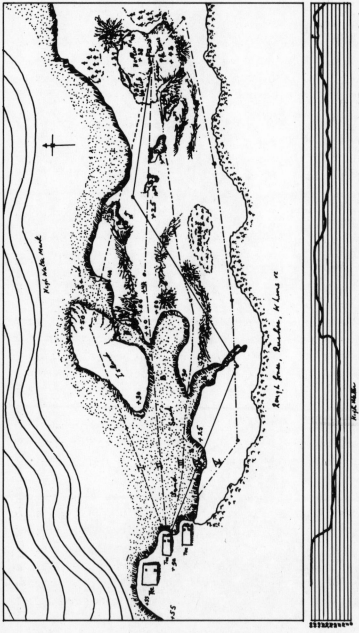

"The ideal two-shot hole that launched my golf architecture career. C.B. Macdonald and Bernard Darwin awarded this design first place in *Country Life* magazine. July 25, 1914."

They are lacking in strategy, as most of them have been designed by architects belonging to the penal school. It is unfortunate that in the Chicago district the best golfing ground, consisting of magnificent sand dune country, is on the south shore bordering the industrial district.

In Detroit also there is some excellent golfing ground— not sand dune country, but nevertheless consisting of bold, pleasing undulations.

⚮ *In California* ⚮

In California there are several outstanding courses. O. B. Keeler goes so far as to say they are so much better than those in the rest of the country that he has no basis of comparison.

California golf courses are of comparatively recent origin. I have been told that before the war there were none in Los Angeles with grass greens, whereas today there are over fifty.

I attribute the excellence of Californian courses to the influence of golf architects like Max Behr and Robert Hunter. I think also that although it has been the fashion to deride Herbert Fowler's efforts, he set a standard which other architects attempted to emulate. It is a great joy to construct golf courses in California, as the Californian sun and hoseless irrigation systems bring up the grasses so quickly that the courses have a springy carpet of turf three months after sowing and give one the impression that they are several years old.

The best of these golf courses are on the Monterey Peninsula. Four courses are already existing and two more are contemplated. We have already discussed Cypress Point. I do not expect anyone will ever have the opportunity of constructing another course like Cypress Point, as I do not suppose anywhere in the world is there such a glorious combination of rocky coast, sand dunes, pine woods and cypress trees.

The Monterey cypress is unique. It has an elbowed

gnarled appearance and is twisted into such fantastic shapes as to be almost frightening. It is even beautiful when dead and the elbowed limbs give the impression of huge white gaunt skeletons of giant men. If one first visits Cypress Point in foggy weather, these weird white skeletons looming out of the mist are so terrifying that they are apt to create a depressing effect which is only dispelled when the sun breaks through the mist and brings to view a wonderful variety of coloring unsurpassed on any golf course. Strange to say, it appears to be impossible to grow the Monterey cypress elsewhere. I have been informed that when an attempt has been made to grow them from seed it has simply resulted in the common garden variety of tree.

⊀ *Pebble Beach* ⊁

When, in 1929, the Amateur Championship was played at Pebble Beach, the course was almost universally admitted to be the best one on which the Championship had been played. It is very beautiful, running along the edge of the coast its whole extent.

The best holes are probably the third, eighth, and eighteenth, the last named being as fine a finish as on any golf course, and it would be better still if the entrance to the green were slightly larger. Considering the magnificence of the terrain, however, the short holes are somewhat disappointing.

The Monterey Peninsula course is considered by many to be as good as Pebble Beach. When it was constructed and ready for seeding, however, it was recognized that it could be vastly improved, and we were called in to alter it. My partner, Robert Hunter, was allowed only thirty days to reconstruct all the greens, and was not permitted to reroute the holes because some of the adjoining lots had been sold, and, consequently, it tied our hands considerably. The ground available for the course was in some respects even better than Cypress Point, and no doubt an equally good

The 8th green at Pebble Beach, which we redesigned.

USGA

169

course might have been constructed if we had been allowed to make it de nove.

The fourth golf course on the Monterey Peninsula is the Del Monte Course. It has always been a complete mystery to me, and is so contrary to my experience in other countries, that it should enjoy such great popularity, which cannot be entirely due to its proximity to the Del Monte Hotel, there being a greater amount of play on it than all the other courses put together. The course is well wooded and is among beautiful surroundings, but the majority of the holes are uninspiring and uninteresting, and it has not even the merit of good greens and fairways.

In London and many other British towns there were many courses of a similar nature to Del Monte, but when newer and better courses were made, such as Sunningdale, Wentworth, and Addington, the majority of the members of the flat park courses deserted them, emigrating elsewhere, and it was not until these park courses were reconstructed that they regained any degree of popularity.

In Scotland, the first question asked on returning to the clubhouse is, "Did you have a good match?" In America, it is only too frequently, "Did you have a good score?"

Scoring is easy at Del Monte, so this may account for its popularity. Since writing this, there has been a marked decrease of play at Del Monte and Pebble Beach, and an increasing amount on the Monterey Peninsula and Cypress Point. Notwithstanding the Depression, last winter Cypress Point had nearly twice as much play as the previous year.

⋆ *Lakeside, Hollywood* ⋆

In Southern California there are many good golf courses. By far the best of these is Max Behr's course at Lakeside, the course on which Bobby Jones played in some of his movie pictures. Lakeside had none of the natural advantages of the Monterey courses, the Olympic at San Francisco or even many of the other courses in the Los Angeles district, but it has been so admirably designed and constructed that it compares favourably with any inland course. It was originally a flattish orchard. Now the whole ground has been made undulating and the undulations have such a natural appearance that they have a close resemblance to real links land.

The interest of the course is entirely due to the undulations and not due to bunkers, which at many of the holes are nonexistent. In a word, Lakeside is one of the world's greatest golf courses.

Norman Macbeth's course, Wilshire, has some interesting holes. The 18th is magnificent. It has not a single bunker, but owes its excellence to a large deep arroyo running diagonally almost the full length of the hole.

On the San Francisco Peninsula there is a wealth of good golfing territory. The sand dune country owned by the Olympic Club, which although not so spectacular as that on the Monterey Peninsula, is the finest golfing territory I have seen in America.

Unfortunately, the courses were designed and constructed at a time when not so much was known about golf course construction as is known today, so that owing to the lack of provision for drainage, floods washed some of the most spectacular holes down the slopes towards the sea.

❧ Sharp Park ❧

The municipal courses in San Francisco are far superior to most municipal courses. The newest, which we constructed at Sharp Park, was made on land reclaimed from the sea, similar to the Lido course; the greens and fairways were built with sand sucked up from below the water. One fairway alone required 200,000 cubic yards of sand to build it up above 10 feet of water. This was probably the biggest engineering feat of its kind that has ever been attempted.

The course now has a great resemblance to real links land. Some of the holes are most spectacular. Two of them are of similar type to the plan of the ideal two-shot holes depicted on page 166. One of them has the island on the right and the other on the left. In designing and constructing the course, we had the greatest assistance from Mr. John Maclaren, the designer of the Golden Gate Park. John Maclaren is an artist, and his help not only in the artistic planting of trees but in creating other delightful features was most valuable.

⚔ *Pasatiempo* ⚔

Miss Marion Hollins was the founder of Pasatiempo, the course at Santa Cruz. My wife and I consider the course so beautiful that we have built a cottage on the edge of the sixth fairway.

I have always wanted to live where one could practice shots in one's pyjamas before breakfast, and at Santa Cruz the climate is so delightful that one can play golf every day in the year, where it is never too hot and never too cold, and if it should rain it usually does so at night.

Many good golfers consider the second nine holes at Pasatiempo the finest in existence. The short holes are specially good, and I think the sixteenth hole is the best two-shot hole I know. I certainly do not know of any hole which gives so great an advantage for length and accuracy.

On the Northern Pacific Coast the best known courses are at Oak Bay and Colwood, Victoria. Oak Bay has an attractive setting by the sea, but if I remember rightly, has three one-shot holes in succession and other defects which prevent it being an ideal course. These defects are largely owing to outcrops of rock which limited the positions available for greens, and when the course was first constructed there was none of the new machinery available for dealing with rock as there is today.

Dr. MacKenzie on the 16th at Pasatiempo—his favorite par 4.

173

Barry Staley

"The sporting 18th at Pasatiempo is truly the magnificent ending due such a delightful round. 135 yards over stupendous hazards and you are on the green. This is not the hole to falter on. Play it bravely." A.M.

❈ *Jasper Park, Canada* ❈

The best known courses in other parts of Canada are Toronto, Hamilton in Ontario, and Jasper Park. Jasper Park has an amazingly beautiful setting surrounded by rock mountains and bordering a lake which is so clear that the reflections of the mountains in it appear more vivid than the mountains themselves. There are some excellent holes on the edge of the lake, and the 18th hole is one of the finest finishes I know.

The whole place is most romantic. Large black bears roam about the course, and on each occasion I played on it one or more came within a short distance and sniffed at us, then walked on.

I played at Jasper Park in the British Senior golfers' team.

When we arrived in Victoria, after the customary dinner, a man gave a most amusing speech and finished up with a story against the British Senior golfers.

    ✄ "When the British Seniors were at Jasper Park, the hotel was kept open a week later than usual in their honor (which was true), so that there were very few people left at the hotel, but there was one young and attractive lady, who, thinking all the British Seniors were out playing golf, considered it would be quite safe to have a bath in the lake in nature's costume. Unfortunately, one of the British Seniors, Little Jimmy, had been playing two rounds of golf a day and was in consequence a bit tired and was not playing that afternoon. When the young lady was ready to dive in the lake she heard a rustling in the bushes behind her. She turned her head and, much alarmed, said, "Who's that?" A little squeaky voice said, "Oh, it's only little Jimmy." "And how old are you, little Jimmy?" she asked, to which a squeaky voice ending in a shriek replied, "I'm eighty-five Gordammit." ✆

There are many other good golf courses in Canada, such as Banff. I recently constructed an additional nine holes at the St. Charles Country Club, Winnipeg, and have had several letters suggesting they are the best nine holes in Canada, but I doubt if this is so, as the terrain was dead flat, adobe soil, devoid of natural features, and it is impossible to make as good a course on land of this description as in other situations where nature has been kinder.

Since writing the above, the Augusta National Bobby Jones Course and Bayside have been completed.

The Augusta National perhaps approaches more closely Bobby Jones' conception of an ideal course than any other, with the possible exception of the Old Course at St. Andrews.

In the *Golfer's Year Book*, Bob Jones states that an ideal golf course must give pleasure to everyone, including the veriest

Bob Jones, Alister MacKenzie and guests testing what will be the 8th hole at Augusta National.

The Life and Times of Bobby Jones

dub. There must always be an alternative route for everyone, and thought should be required as well as mechanical skill, and above all it should never be hopeless for the duffer, nor fail to concern and interest the expert.

Bayside also very closely approaches his conception of an ideal course. Unlike the Augusta National, it was devoid of natural features and everything had to be artificially constructed. It has only 19 bunkers, whereas the Augusta National has twenty-two.

As an indication of its great popularity even in these depressed times, the owners have taken in over $10,000 each playing month in green fees—probably more than twice as much as any of the other public courses in New York State. Bayside is a proof that even in these depressed times, if a golf course is constructed on ideal lines, it will pay.

The rock bottom test of an ideal golf course or hole is not one that enjoys a temporary popularity, but one that lives.

The 8th green at Cruden Bay. The sheep will be observed keeping the fairways.

178

❧5❧
Greenkeeping

Errors in greenkeeping not infrequently arise from a misconception of what is required for a golf course. Agricultural experts, green committees and greenkeepers often make the mistake of treating turf for playing fields on similar lines to that required for feeding cattle.

Even Drs. Piper and Oakley, who have done so much to put greenkeeping on a scientific basis, in their earlier experiments, as evidenced by their book *Turf for Golf Courses*, made this mistake. The truth is that golf courses and other playing fields require grasses with a thick matted root growth and a dwarf leaf—grasses which require little mowing and provide a firm springy carpet that is a pleasure to walk on.

On the other hand, from an agricultural point of view, the most desirable grasses have a small root growth and a large succulent leaf.

The former grasses grow naturally on virgin soil, preferably of a sour, peaty or sandy nature, whereas agricultural grasses require a rich sweet soil of an alkaline reaction.

It is an easy matter by means of lime, basic slag or alkaline fertilizers to convert soil which is producing the finest golfing grasses into that which is favourable to the growth of rich, succulent agricultural grasses, clover and weeds, but it is amazingly difficult to reverse the process. On scores of occasions I have known magnificent golfing turf ruined by the expenditure of a few dollars on alkaline fertilizers. An alkaline condition of the soil also encourages worms and their attendant evils.

To restore the finer golfing grasses which have been destroyed by injudicious treatment requires years of labour and the expenditure of thousands of dollars in weed and worm killers, nitrogenous fertilizers, top dressings and seeds. Most golf clubs have enough money to destroy existing turf, but few, if any, have sufficient funds to restore it again.

As I have already mentioned, I was the founder of Alwoodley Golf Club, and its architect nearly thirty years ago. For over twenty years the course was kept up by five men or less, and the greens and fairways were considered unequalled in England. The grasses on the fairways were of such a slow growing character that they often did not require mowing more than three times a year. These excellent results were not obtained by spending money, but by refusing to do so.

In the early stages of the existence of the course, part of the land consisted of rich agricultural grasses, daisies and weeds, which have gradually disappeared and been replaced by dwarf golfing grasses. This has been due to constant mowing and leaving the cut grass on to nourish the soil. In this connection it is astonishing how few greenkeepers realize that the best fertilizer for the finer grass is grass itself.

When the Alwoodley course was constructed, although I had some slight knowledge of chemistry, I knew little about the science of agriculture or botany. I felt instinctively, however (or was it perhaps by observation of moorland, public commons or links land?), that when grass land was treated by agriculturalists the turf invariably became unsuitable for playing fields. I therefore determined to resist any attempts by the green committee or greenkeeper to fertilize Alwoodley unless there were some definite reason for doing so.

On several occasions, attempts were made by some member of the club who owned a farm or garden to persuade us to use lime, basic slag, kinit, or some alkaline fertilizer, but up to the present time we have successfully resisted them.

It is of importance that greenkeepers realize that the fundamental principle of successful greenkeeping is the recognition of the fact that the finest golfing grasses flourish on poor soil and that more harm is done by over-, rather than underfertilizing. It is true that, owing to the fact that grass cuttings are being continually removed from the greens, some compost or other fertilizer is necessary to replace their loss, but provided there is already a good carpet of turf, feeding is rarely required on fairways.

It is not even necessary that fairways should consist entirely of grasses. There should be a freedom from clover, daisies and plantains, dandelions and other weeds, but others such as yarrow, chickweed, perlwort, moss, and in Britain patches of closely cut heather, make excellent fairways. It is also pleasing to the eye to have varying shades of green instead of one uniform colour.

It is possible to have too high a degree of perfection.

⊀ I remember many years ago at Sunningdale a fussy oily individual coming up to Harry Colt and saying, "I really must congratulate you, Mr. Colt, on your fairways. They are perfect." Colt, who objected to this type of man, answered somewhat testily, "I don't agree with you at all." "Why not, Mr. Colt?" he asked. "The lies are too damned good," was the answer. ⊁

There is a certain amount of truth in this. If we have never had a bad lie we are not likely to appreciate a good one, and moreover, the ability to play from a bad lie differentiates between a good player and a bad one. We might also remark that good and bad lies differentiate between good sportsmen and bad.

If you want to find out if a man is a good trustworthy fellow or not, play golf with him.

The Life and Times of Bobby Jones

Jones hosting his distinguished guests at Augusta National.

I have already pointed out that in the old days in Scotland the best golf courses were those kept by the rabbits. When these courses became popular and attracted English and American visitors, they deteriorated in proportion to the additional amount of money expended on them.

One of the first principles in greenkeeping is never to expend a penny on a golf course unless you are absolutely certain that the money expended is going to do good and not harm to the course. Similar principles apply to any new construction work on a golf course. No new hazards should ever be added to a golf course unless you are satisfied that they are going to make the course more interesting and exciting.

In my lectures of twenty years ago I pointed out that on most golf courses there are far too many bunkers, and that the only object of bunkers is to make golf courses more interesting, or, in other words, more popular. Since then I am more convinced than ever that no bunker should be constructed unless one is convinced that it will make a course more pleasurable.

For example, on Bob Jones' new course, the Augusta National, I had originally planned thirty-six bunkers. I took my map to Bob, who thoroughly agrees with my ideas, as evidenced by his article on his "Ideal Golf Course" in the *Golfer's Year Book*, and I suggested to him that some of the bunkers had no meaning and might be eliminated. We reduced them to twenty-two, and yet Bob thinks we have made the most interesting test of golf in America.

We have already pointed out that it would be wise for every club to have a permanent green committee. The history of most clubs is that a green committee is appointed who make mistakes. Just as they are beginning to learn from experience of their mistakes, they are replaced by fresh members who make still greater ones.

On the other hand, some clubs with which I have been associated have in their early stages passed a resolution that no changes will be made to the course except on the advice of the original architect or one of equal reputation, and as a result these courses have continued to improve year by year.

183

In a former chapter it has been suggested that in the nature of things no changes to a golf course originated by a green committee in consultation with a professional or greenkeeper can ever be a complete success. The only exceptions I have known to this rule when any real improvement resulted have been when the committee has been dominated by some benevolent autocrat who has made a lifelong study of the subject. Woking and John L. Low, Sunningdale and Harry Colt, and the Merion Cricket Club and the Wilson Brothers are cases in point.

Only a short time ago I was playing on a course owned by perhaps the richest club in Northern California. Extensive alterations were being made to it on the advice of the local professional. If these alterations had been made from the point of view of annoying and harassing the average member of the club, they would have been most effective, but from the standpoint of interest it would have been better if the money expended had been thrown into the sea.

If a course on real links land comes into your hands, let well enough alone and do not make any alterations except after the most careful consideration and expert advice.

The expression "come into your hands" suggests one of the best stories I ever saw in *Punch*.

✺ Four Cockney veterans were returning to London in a railway carriage from France during the war. They were showing each other their souvenirs, but one dour old boy in the corner took little notice until one of the others turned to him and said " 'Aven't you got no souvenirs or nuffink?" "Naow" he said "Wot do I want wiv a souvenir? Wot's the good of an 'elmet if yer gets yer 'ead blown orf in tryin' ter git it? Wot's the good of an 'elmet wivout an 'ead ter put it on?" Then one of the others said, "But if a souvenir came into yer 'and wouldn't yer 'ave it?" "Well," he said, "If it come into me 'and it's a different matter." Then he felt in his pocket and brought out a door knocker and said, "This 'ere came into me 'and and I'll just tell yer 'ow it 'appened. It was in Wipers [Ypres], and Wipers was not then as it is naow, there were a few 'ouses abaht. One very dark night I saw wot them Frenchies calls an Est-aminet. The beer is not like our beer but its wet anywie, so I went up to the 'ouse and got 'old of the door knocker and gives it a biff but nuffin 'appened and I was just goin' ter give it anuvver biff when up comes a Jack Johnson [a high explosive shell] an' blew the bloomin' 'ouse out o' me 'and." ❧

One cannot emphasize too frequently the importance of leaving God's gifts alone and never fertilizing unless it is certain that time and nature will fail to cure. The researches of the Advisory Green Section of the United States Golf Association have simplified to a most amazing degree the problems of greenkeeping, but the Green Section would be the first to admit that it is a subject which is still in its infancy and that they are continually learning through their mistakes, varied experiences, and scientific research.

I have already stated that at first mistakes were made of treating golfing turf on similar lines to that required for feeding cattle. Views have changed, and it is now recognized that in distinction to the treatment of land required for agriculture it was essential to treat golfing turf with fertilizers which tended to create an acidity of the soil. The result of this treatment was to produce turf consisting of delicate dwarf grasses, and more remarkable still, to create a soil in which daisies, plantains, clover and many obnoxious weed seeds refuse to germinate.

Scientific research and the experience gleaned from our mistakes is the only way we shall solve these problems, so that the more money provided for the Green Section to continue their researches the sooner we shall arrive at the truth of the matter. The Green Section should be allowed sufficient money not only to conduct experimental stations in different parts of America, but also to enable them to play golf and to study courses all over the world.

If the advisory members had the opportunity of playing and absorbing the spirit of golf on some of the old classical courses such as St. Andrews, they would view the requirements of the game in its true perspective. They would find, for example, that the treatment for the approaches is almost as important as that for the greens, and that one of, if not *the* most fascinating of shots, is the run up approach we so frequently get on old seaside courses like St. Andrews. An approach of this kind cannot be made successfully if there is a defined margin between the approach and the green, or if the approaches and greens are kept so soggy with water that no other shot is possible except an inartistic pitch. They would also find that not only is a complete sward of grass on the fairways unnecessary but not even desirable.

Certain weeds and mosses make excellent fairways, and there is great beauty in scarlet pimpernels and other dwarf flowers. Even bunches of white flowers of the despised chickweeds make a beautiful setting on the edge of bunkers.

I have an old friend who is perhaps the greatest authority on public parks in America, who is frequently expressing his preference for grass that is green. The best golfing grasses vary in colour. They may be red, brown, blue, dark green, light green, yellow and at times even white and gray.

A golf course that consisted entirely of one shade of green would be merely ugly. There is great charm and beauty in the varying shades of colour of a golf course.

Many years ago I wrote some articles on greenkeeping. Experience in advising over four hundred golf clubs has modified my views but has not entirely changed the general principles which I held originally.

A common mistake in greenkeeping is to imagine that because one form of treatment benefits one course that it will necessarily benefit another. The greenkeeper should have sufficient knowledge of chemistry and botany to be able to tell what form of treatment is most likely to benefit his particular greens.

A common mistake is not to mow greens during winter months. I have not the slightest doubt that mowing greens during winter months is beneficial to them. It keeps the grass from becoming coarse. On those Scottish courses where the greens are so good all through the winter, are not the rabbits mowing the greens all through those winter months with their teeth? Are the knives of the mowing machines likely to do the grass harm when the teeth of the rabbits do it good?

By introducing labour saving machinery we have recently been getting better results at a much lower cost. If work on a large scale is being done, the steam navvy or grab might be used for excavating or making hummocks; traction engines are useful in uprooting small trees, and larger ones with advantage can be blown up by dynamite. I recently used blasting charges for making bunkers. An article in one of the Sheffield papers somewhat humorously stated that this was not the first occasion when Dr. MacKenzie's bunkers had been "blasted."

It is advisable to drain golfing ground much more thoroughly and efficiently than ordinary farmland, but on the other hand, by exercising a little thought it can be done much more cheaply. For golfing purposes, it is not only unnecessary to drain as deeply as is customary for agricultural purposes, but it is much cheaper and more satisfactory to adopt a system of shallow drains.

On a golf course there is rarely any need to make allowance for the necessity of subsoil ploughing; the drains can therefore be kept near the surface. The great thing to bear in mind about draining is that the water stratum must be tapped.

On heavy clay land, it is absurd to put drains in the middle of the clay unless the whole of the trench is filled in with clinkers or other porous material, and this is needless expense. Drains may at times be placed in a groove on the surface of the clay. On land of this description they may often be placed with advantage at as shallow a depth as from six to twelve inches. It should be unnecessary to state that no effort should be spared to see that there is sufficient fall,

MacKenzie blasting from his own bunker at the 12th at Pasatiempo.

Barry Staley

and for the purpose of ensuring this it is often necessary to take levels.

Sufficient thought is rarely given to drainage. The site of the main drains and the whole scheme of drainage should be very carefully studied, and it is of special importance to take into consideration the nature of the subsoil and position of the water level.

The cheapest method of draining is by a system of mole drainage. I have frequently used a mole drain worked by horses which was made from ideas evolved by Franks—the Moortown greenkeeper—and myself. It is used as an attachment to the turf cutting machine.

In my experience it is frequently not a difficult matter to get excellent turf in the immediate neighborhood of a golf course at an extremely cheap rate, and the added advantage is that turf obtained from the immediate vicinity of the course is much more likely to be suitable than turf obtained from elsewhere.

It should be borne in mind that the most useless turf from a farming point of view is frequently the most valuable for golf.

There are many other details which lessen the cost of turfing. In an old-established course, turf for new greens or for renovating old ones can frequently be obtained from the sides of a neighboring fairway, the sods from which may be replaced by those removed from the site of the green.

There is usually a well-trodden path extending from every tee to the nearest fairway. There is no turf so useful for renovating an old tee, or making a new one, as that obtained from a firm path of this kind. The sods removed should be replaced by others, and they in turn get hard and firm.

Although the best time to turf is in the late autumn and winter months, sods can, if necessity arises, be laid in certain localities as late as June. If hot dry weather arrives, the newly laid sods should be covered with cut grass during the day, and in the evening the grass should be removed so that the dews help to keep the ground moist.

MacKenzie, Hollins, H.J. Wigham and Hunter before seeding of a fairway.

⚜ *Seeding* ⚜

I have known of several instances where ground has been sown and the result has been so unsatisfactory that after a year or two the ground has been ploughed up and re-sown. It is much more economical in the long run to do the thing thoroughly. Mistakes are most frequently made in sowing with the wrong seeds, in not preparing the ground thoroughly beforehand and in sowing at the wrong time of year.

It is most important that a mixture should be chosen containing a goodly proportion of seeds corresponding to the prevailing grasses of the neighborhood, and seeds should always be obtained from a seeds merchant who is not afraid of telling you the exact composition of the mixture.

Some seeds merchants sell mixtures which are not so good for golfing grass as they appear. It is not the best kind of grass which germinates too quickly. Finer turf usually results from a mixture which comes up more slowly but is of a more permanent character. If seeding is necessary, it is frequently advisable to sow with much larger quantity of seed than is customary. It is of the utmost importance to prepare the land thoroughly before seeding. It should be well-drained, the land well-limed when necessary, and fifteen loads to the acre of well-rotted stable manure incorporated in the soil, or a mixture of artificial manure in its stead.

After sowing, see that the birds are scared away by one of the numerous devices suggested for the purpose.

⚜ *Manures* ⚜

Manures should be used with a considerable amount of discretion and only in small quantities at a time.

It is surprising how much money can be saved in

manures by the help of science and a sufficient knowledge of chemistry to enable you to judge which are the cheapest and most valuable manures suitable for the soil of the locality with which you have to deal.

I have known a considerable amount of damage done by the indiscriminate use of artificial manures. For example, artificials are of the greatest possible value for golfing turf, but they should always be used frequently in small quantities and should be well-diluted with soil or sand, and only used during moist weather.

A greenkeeper should attempt to get a sufficient knowledge of botany and chemistry to know by the character of the herbage of his greens the kind and amount of manure required. Greenkeepers sometimes think that if they use twice the usual quantity of a manure, it will have double the effect. The exact contrary is the case, as the green may be entirely ruined.

The most important manure of all is cut grass. If the cut grass is always left on the greens and fairways, very little manuring is necessary. On the other hand, if the grass is constantly removed year after year, unless a considerable amount of manure is added to take its place, the turf becomes impoverished and full of weeds.

❧ *Sand* ❧

Sand is often an expensive item on an inland course. It is surprising how frequently a good class of sand is found in pockets on a course or in the immediate vicinity. A knowledge of geology or botany may enable you to foretell the most likely places. On several occasions on visiting a course, I have been told that there was no sand in the district and have been able to find some by noting the character of the trees and grasses.

Sand may be economized by the method in which bunkers are made. It will be noticed in the photographs reproduced that most of the hollows have been turfed but have been formed in such a way that a ball gravitates towards the sand, which is thrown up against its face.

Bunkers of this description have a much more natural appearance, and the amount of sand needed is considerably less than usual.

By far the most important of all the foregoing suggestions is the ultimate economy of making it as reasonably certain as possible that any work done is of a permanent character and has not, ultimately, to be done over again.

There are few committees of golf clubs who attach sufficient importance to expert advice. I suppose this is due partly to the fact that they themselves would sooner have the work done badly and have the fun of doing it than see anyone else do it for them. In the nature of things a course can only be constructed by an individual.

"Too many cooks spoil the broth" is a proverb which is more applicable in the case of golf courses than anything else. Personally, I am a strong believer in encouraging the individuality of the greenkeeper and not interfering with, but rather encouraging, his original ideas unless they are in opposition to sound fundamental principles.

These views were expressed nearly twenty years ago regarding my experience of British courses.

❈ *Soil* ❧

Further investigations and experience have on the whole confirmed my views on fertilizers expressed so many years ago.

It would be difficult to emphasize too strongly the importance of treating turf for golf entirely differently to that suitable for agriculture. If you are fortunate enough to have fairways as we had at Alwoodley, which only require mowing about three times a year, why fertilize it and have to mow it four times a week?

Injudicious use of sulphate of ammonia or any other fertilizer not only may cause irreparable damage to a course, but in any case will require some other chemical to neutralize its ill effects.

In this respect the treatment of golf courses is similar to that for human beings. The best physicians are those who only prescribe poisonous drugs after the most careful consideration.

I often think there is no preliminary training so useful in the treatment of golf courses as that of the medical man. Not only is his knowledge of chemistry, botany, biology, physiology, bacteriology and so on of value, but of far greater importance is the mental training which prevents him interfering with nature and never using the drastic measures of the knife if a cure can be obtained by simple means.

Modern medicine consists largely in discovering the causes of disease and supplying what is lacking in the human body, such as extracts of the thyroid, pancreas, adrenal and other glands. Similarly, in greenkeeping no treatment is required if nature can effect a cure, the knife should be avoided if better and more permanent results can be obtained by simpler means, and no drugs should be used except those necessary to replace constituents in the soil that are lacking and retarding the growth of the finer golfing grasses.

Nitrogen is the most important food for golfing grasses, but in providing nitrogen it is important not to get too great a degree of acidity.

At Cypress Point we were much distressed because the soil on the proposed fairways on the coast showed a high degree of alkalinity. We were afraid that Agrostis maritima (seaside bent) might not do well on such highly alkaline soil, so before seeding we added a considerable amount of sulphur, and since then we have used frequent dressings of sulphate of ammonia. To our astonishment, the fairways near the coast are as perfect as any we have seen. The Agrostis maritima has dominated all the other grasses and there is not a weed or a leaf of clover to be seen anywhere.

Virgin soil, or soil that has been uncultivated for many years, always makes the best golfing land.

The word "links" originally denoted open uncultivated land. Cypress Point was constructed on virgin land. The pH varied from 4.5 to 8.4. Although most of the land was rich in nitrogen, the richest was where the pH was highest. It is probably owing to this excess of nitrogen that we have been able to obtain fairways and greens that are generally considered to compare favourably with any in the world.

During recent years the one-horse scraper has been superseded by the Fresno scraper and four horses, and this has been superseded in its turn by the sixty-horsepower caterpillar with scraper and bulldozer attachment. These new machines do contouring work in certain kinds of soils at less than half the cost of the Fresno and probably less than a quarter of the cost of the old scoop.

Thirty years ago labour in Britain could be obtained for four pence (eight cents) an hour, and all golf courses were constructed by hand labour. Today, notwithstanding that wages are higher, having risen manyfold, yet much better results can be obtained at a much lower cost than before.

It is largely due to the influence of America that progress in the use of labour saving machinery has been gained, so that the world owes Americans an infinite amount of gratitude for the introduction of these wealth producing machines which are the secret of high wages, full employment and prosperity for all.

There are a few points in regard to drainage I would like to emphasize, and others which I would like to modify. It is very important that the water stratum should be tapped. For example, if a hard pan is present it is essential that this be broken up and the drain tiles placed below the upper level of the hard pan.

It will have been noted in my old writings that I advocated, from the point of view of economy, shallow drainage in clay land. The reason I did so was because in Britain nearly a hundred years ago the government gave a subsidy to farmers for drainage on condition that the drains were laid over four feet deep. In clay land most of these drains are dry and useless up to this day. On the other hand if they had been filled with some porous material they would have been valuable.

Further experience has taught me that it is not wise to advocate shallow drains. The drain tiles are only too likely to get blocked or broken, and this is particularly so if mole drainage is used to supplement the tile drainage. An important thing which is often overlooked in tile drainage is that the water flows into the pipes through the bottom and not through the tops and sides. Sand and other sediment can therefore be prevented from blocking the pipes by covering the upper two-thirds of the junctions between the pipes with some impervious material without interfering with the flow of the water. Covering the upper two-thirds with concrete is especially valuable in drain pipes running through sand hazards.

It has already been pointed out that the drainage of a golf course is facilitated by the manner in which the construction is carried out.

On all our recent golf courses on flattish land we have designed a series of swales which not only assist the drainage but give us plenty of earth to make the greens, hillocks, undulating ground and so on. The swales will take care of the storm water, and small pipes at the bottom of them will drain off any small pockets of water which remain. When a course is constructed in this way the expense of tile drains is often unnecessary.

In the construction of a golf course, this principle of swales communicating with deeper ones should be extended to all hollows in greens, approaches, bunkers and any other communications wherever possible.

Up to the last few years I had little experience in seeding. In Britain, partly owing to the difficulty in obtaining reliable seed, better and cheaper results were obtained by turfing the greens and fertilizing the fairways and allowing the natural grasses to come up. In America, however, there is no difficulty about getting reliable seed, although it is wise to have it thoroughly tested before use.

One seeds merchant quoted us Agrostis maritima at a very low figure for Cypress Point. We had it tested and found it to contain nothing but red top.

If time will permit, it is also desirable to have experimental plots to test the effects of different fertilizers, and the influence of different soils on the germination of varying seeds. It is also advisable to obtain a clean seed bed by continually turning over the soil and exposing it to the sun to kill the weed seeds.

At the Meadow Club at Mount Tamalpais we turned over the soil more than six times before obtaining a clean seed bed. Taking into consideration that before seeding there was nothing but weeds, it is remarkably free from them today.

After obtaining a clean seed bed, the greatest preventative of weeds and clover is—with the aid of the sun, water, fertilizers and suitable seed—to bring up such a rapid growth of turf that there is no room for weeds to exist.

The kind of water used for irrigation is also of great importance. Irrigation may deposit an enormous amount of undesirable salts during the year, so that it is advisable in the choice of seed to be guided not only by the soil but also by the character of the water.

At Sharp Park, San Francisco's new municipal course, the well water contained as large a proportion of common salt as seven hundred parts per million. As it was obvious that few grasses would flourish under these conditions, after the most careful inquiries we used seed, Agrostis maritima, from Marshfield Oregon which we knew was flooded with sea water two months each year, and we omitted the Poa trivialis, Pratensis and the fescues which at one time we thought would be desirable.

At Pasatiempo, Santa Cruz, the fairways were nearly free from clover for the first few months, but during the winter they became covered with it. We attributed this to the excessive amount of carbonate of lime in the water, and thought

The beautiful Meadow Club at Tamalpais.

it would be a great expense to get rid of it by picking it by hand and using nitrogenous fertilizers. Fortunately we discovered a weed puller invented by a man in Santa Cruz from whom Miss Marion Hollins bought the patent. This weed puller is shaped like a rake with large claws set at an angle so that it grasps the clover and other weeds, but allows the grasses to slip through its fingers. With these weed pullers we got rid of the clover on the first and ninth fairways in three days. One man and one weed puller doing the work of more than fifteen men by ordinary methods.

In Britain we are not troubled with water problems, except too much of it, but in California and other American states the expense of irrigation and upkeep is a serious problem. A first class irrigation system is a specialist's job. There are few engineers who are capable of designing a system as at Pasatiempo where all the fairway watering can be done by one man. A still more difficult problem is the effect on the vegetation of the water used. I have searched the bulletins of the U.S.G.A. and other sources, but can find very little written on the subject.

It would be of great interest if the Advisory Committee of the Green Section would make further investigations on the influence of varying water supplies on grasses and weeds.

At Cypress Point we have the finest fairways I know of anywhere, but our water bill is enormous. It is possible we could save the excessive amount by sinking wells on the property, but is it worthwhile risking the possibility of the well water doing irreparable damage and might it not be better to continue using the water we know suits our turf, notwithstanding its great expense? If the Green Section were able by their experiments to solve our difficulties, they would save us thousands of dollars a year.

We had excellent results from so-called Astoria bent from Oregon on the Union League (Greenhills) course at San Francisco, but our experience is limited so we cannot express any dogmatic views on the subject. Agrostis maritima and Astoria bent have not the same tendency to creep as Washington Metropolitan and other bents planted by vegetative methods, so they do not necessitate the same expense in wire brushing, but the finest greens are those consisting of Agrostis canina.

The time may come when it is possible to obtain a pure seed at a reasonable cost, and then this may supersede all other grasses. Chewings and other fescues make beautiful greens, but I do not know of any fescue that will stand close mowing for more than a year or two. On the other hand, fescues do much better on fairways where the mowing machines do not cut so closely, and on soil that is suitable for them they give more perfect fairways than any other grass.

A good greenkeeper keeps a careful watch on his turf, and has sleepless nights until he has overcome everything that may be the matter with it. The best greenkeepers are not necessarily those trained in Scotland—they are invariably honest, hardworking, and reliable, but not always receptive of new ideas. On the other hand, Scotsmen who

Barry Staley

Cyril Tolley, Marion Hollins, Bobby Jones and Glenna Collet at the opening of Pasatiempo.

15th Green – Union League Golf Club.

16490

View from the 15th green. A two-tiered green at Union League (Green Hills) with a strong carry of 155 yards over the canyon.

Green Hills

are learning de novo and have not been spoilt by stereotyped methods of greenkeeping are excellent. Some of the best greenkeepers I have known have been Irishmen.

⋈ I heard a story of one of them who was ill in the hospital as the result of liquor. The priest called to see him when he was convalescent, and as he was departing he leaned over the bed and said "Now Pathric that ye're lavin' the hospital I hope you'll lead a dacent and a sobre loife." Voice from the bed: "What's that, Father?" "Now Pathric that ye're lavin' the hospital I hope that ye'll lead a dacent and sobre loife." Voice from the bed: "A little nearer, Father." "Now Pathric—ye're not deaf are ye Pathric?" "No, but Oi've been lyin' on me back and haven't touched a drop o' the Cratur for four weeks and your breath is loike (deep inspiration) the breath of heaven." ⋈

There are a few more points in economical greenkeeping I would like to emphasize.

A first class greenkeeper will reduce hand labour to a minimum. He will insist on the best mowing machines and see that they are kept in order. He will arrange that all banks and hollows are cut with a power machine and if the slopes are too abrupt to allow of this being done readily he will urge the green committee to take steps to have the course reconstructed.

Similarly, if the irrigation system requires more than one man, he should urge that an up-to-date hoseless system be introduced. After the first few years, the upkeep of a golf course in Britain should rarely require more than five and in America not more than eight men to keep it in perfect condition.

As things are, it is only on rare occasions that one finds a course kept perfectly with as large a number as fifteen or twenty men. How many courses are there where the approaches are cut so that they merge imperceptibly into the greens? How many are free from long grass and the accompanying annoyance of lost balls? How many are free from clover and weeds, not only on the greens but on the fairways?

Many clubs spend far too much money in doing unnecessary things. Sometimes one finds long grass being cut with scythes; on many courses there is much too large a bunker acreage to keep up. During recent years there have been many clubs who have raked their bunkers deeply so that only a niblick shot was possible out of them. This does not make for good or interesting golf. It merely makes for monotony and reduces everyone to the same level, preventing an expert player from showing his judgment and skill in the choice of clubs in recovering from bunkers, and preventing him from ever having the joy of making a spectacular recovery with a full brassy shot.

It is essential that a greenkeeper should grasp the fundamental principles, and above all realize that golf is a game and that it is played for fun.

❧ A chairman of the Green Committee said to his greenkeeper, "Murphy, I have just been told that a man drove the stream at the 13th hole." "Whoi, that's impossible. Braid and Vardon and Hagen and Bobby Jones have all played the 13th hole an' not wan o' them cud do ut. There is not wan o' them cud git into ut." "Well, maybe you're right," said the chairman, "but I heard it was your boy Dan." "Oh," he said, "Danny could do ut." ❧

In memory of Alister MacKenzie, designer of Pasatiempo Golf Course.

❖6❖

In the Seventies at Sixty

It is not an unusual thing to break eighty at sixty years of age, but it is exceptional after more than forty years of golf to break eighty for the first time at sixty and continue to do so fairly consistently.

I have often thought that the average golfer would gain far more assistance in learning the game of golf from someone who has suffered from all the agonies of the dub and has finally conquered his troubles, than from one of the leading players who has been born with a natural swing or has acquired one in his youth by a subconscious imitation of one or more of the best golfers and who, in consequence, has never suffered from any of the mistakes that plague the life of the long handicap player.

I have also thought that a man who has had a training in anatomy and who knows the functions of the joints and muscles, has a knowledge of the influence of the mind in controlling the movements of these joints and, in addition, has a sound conception of the mechanics of the golf swing and the flight of the golf ball, would be better able to impart his knowledge than someone who has had no such training.

I first commenced to play golf in Scotland when I was about eighteen years of age. At that time I described it as a

"Dr. MacKenzie is the most improved player around Pasatiempo these days. Although not a long hitter, he uses splendid judgment and is now shooting the course consistently in the low eighties. He recently made an eagle two on the difficult par 4 seventh hole."—*Santa Cruz Sentinel*

rotten game, that you simply smote a ball as hard as you could and then spent half an hour looking for it.

I did not take it up again seriously until nearly ten years later, and I then developed the disease badly. I read every book—or almost every book—that had been written on the subject. I had lessons or heard the theories of most of the leading players. I watched them, studied them, thought I had the secret scores of times but it had always eluded me. The fact of the matter is that anything, however silly it may be, that gives one confidence, has the effect of causing a temporary improvement in one's game.

Many times I have thought that my medical training might be of value in describing the golf swing, and scores of times I had decided to write my views, but just as I was about to do so the secret had gone and shortly afterwards been replaced by something else equally absurd.

This has occurred so often that I finally made up my mind that I would never do anything so foolish as to put any theories on paper until I had held the same views for at least twelve months. I have now held them for some years, and except for temporary lapses in putting, notwithstanding increasing age, my game has continued to improve every month.

I now believe that the results of my investigations cannot fail to improve the game of all golfers, and particularly those who have suffered as I have suffered in the past. The improvement in my game has been largely due to the two Joneses: Ernest Jones, and Robert Tyre Jones, Jr.

❧ In this connection I am reminded of an incident which occurred when I was with Bob Jones in Hollywood when he was making his second group of pictures for Warner Brothers. A lady golfer, a friend of mine, was also there, and the day before the competition at the Los Angeles Country Club she told Bob Jones she was feeling so ill that she did not think she would be able to play. Bob Jones said, "I have some medicine which may do you a bit of good," and he sent her a bottle of Teacher's Whiskey. The following evening after she had broken the women's

Ernest Jones—one of golf's greatest teachers.

record of the course he received a note from her. "Three great teachers, Bob Jones, Ernest Jones and Teacher's Whiskey. Result 74." ✦

Several years ago I first met Ernest Jones, professional of the Women's National and of the Pasatiempo Club, Santa Cruz, California during the winter months. Knowing his great reputation as a teacher, I asked him, "What is the secret of the golf swing?" Jones assured me that there was no secret. "Can a boy tell you how he throws a stone?" he said. "If you ask him he will simply say 'I throw it like this.' He neither thinks about it nor can he explain the movements of his knees, hips, shoulders, or wrist joints, and if he began to think about these things it would surely have the effect of hampering his movements."

John O. London quotes a verse from a poem which is a happy illustration of this:

The Centipede was happy quite
Until a Toad in fun
Said "Pray which leg goes over which?"
This put his mind in such a pitch
He lay distracted in a ditch
Considering how to run.

Ernest Jones' teaching consists in three words and three words only: "Swing club head." By club head he does not mean the shaft or the handle of the club, but the *head* of the club. He believes that if one gets a correct mental picture of swinging the club head like a weight at the end of a string the necessary body movements will automatically adjust themselves.

Ernest Jones' teaching is entirely positive, whereas the teaching of others is largely negative. When Jones is giving a lesson you will hear him repeat hundreds of times, "the club head," "the head, the head."

An onlooker may remark that the pupil is not pivoting correctly or his wrists are wrong, his left arm is bent at the

209

top of the swing, he is moving his head, he is not following through, he is pressing and not timing his shots and so on. Jones' invariable reply is, "He is doing all those things and a hundred others as well but DON'T LET HIM KNOW ABOUT IT. If a player concentrates on the movements of the hip or any other joint that assists in propelling the club head smoothly and rapidly, it will destroy all smoothness of rhythm and he never will be able to swing his club head properly."

Jones' argument is that no man can possibly think of more than one thing in one given moment of time, and if he concentrates on swinging his club head smoothly in the largest possible arc of a circle all his mistakes will be rectified.

His pupil does after a time swing his club head and then everything comes right in a miraculous manner. He pivots perfectly, his head remains still, his left arm becomes straight at the top of the swing, he develops a fine follow-through and his timing is perfect.

When Jones first gave me a lesson, I told him I would never be able to swing a club because during my football days I had broken a bone in my left wrist which had never united. He replied, "I've only one leg but that does not prevent my swinging one."

Ernest Jones lost his leg during the war, and on his return home he startled everyone by going round his home course, Chislehurst, with one leg, in 62, thus breaking the record by several strokes. The length and accuracy of his drive on one leg might, at first, make one somewhat skeptical as to the theories enunciated so frequently of late regarding the importance of the hip movements in the golf swing. It is nevertheless true, as George Beldam pointed out many years ago, that an analysis of slow motion pictures proves that the best players start the golf swing with a movement of the hips, and this preliminary movement results in the club head being left behind at the commencement of the swing. Beldam termed this the flail movement. It should occur naturally in the effort to start the club head in motion, and any volitional attempt to introduce it can only result in failure.

I can speak with a certain amount of authority on this subject, as at one time I was obsessed with Beldam's theory and it had such a detrimental effect on my game that my handicap went up several strokes. It has taken Ernest Jones many hours of reiteration of "feel the club head" to cure me of the faults in my swing resulting from it.

Ernest Jones is perhaps the world's most successful teacher. The success of the American Women's Team against the British in 1932 may be attributed to his coaching of Virginia Van Wie and some of the other members of the team.

There is a great deal in his theories, and in particular regarding the detrimental effects on one's game of an analysis of the golf swing.

Is there a single one of the champion golfers who read or was taught anything about the theory of the game before he started to swing a golf club? Most of them will tell you that even to this day they have never read a book on the subject. Without exception they all developed a natural style by swinging at a golf ball in their youth. There may have been some subconscious imitation of the swing of a good player, but no more than might be expected from imitative youth.

Enamored as I am of Jones' theories, and fully aware of the good he has done in emphasizing the fact that it is the head of the club with which one hits the ball, just as in casting a fly it is the tip of the rod with which one casts the line, nevertheless I am convinced that a clear conception of the fundamentals of the golf swing is a considerable help in enabling one to propel a ball with greater and greater accuracy and power.

Even though I deprecate an overanalysis of the golf swing, and although I thoroughly agree that the teaching of golf should be positive and not negative—as it is worse than useless to emphasize a mistake when one is suffering from scores of them—yet I think a knowledge of the mechanics of the golf swing is helpful in still further improving the game of anyone who has grasped the fundamental fact that swinging the club head is of primary importance.

Let me quote an example to show that whereas the swinging of the club head is the basis of a good shot, yet it is not the final word. Last year I played golf with Bobby Jones on several occasions, and one night he, Victor East and I were discussing the golf swing until three in the morning. They both told me that I was swinging easily but I gave them the impression that I was overemphasizing the importance of swinging the club head smoothly and that I was not getting sufficient power and length. They said I was rotating my wrists at the commencement of the backswing and this had the effect of preventing my getting all the power of the muscles at the back of the left shoulder into the shot.

I told them I had always understood that a certain degree of the rotation of the wrists was essential, and they explained that it was the body which rotated and not the wrists.

I have proved subsequently that they were right, and have lengthened my drive forty or fifty yards in consequence.

I shall have more to say about this later on, but for the present my point is that no amount of reiteration of "swing the club head" could have cured me of this fault, whereas a knowledge of the mechanics of the golf swing would have done so.

Many writers on the golf swing use anatomical terms such as pronation, supination and so on, but I do not think I have ever seen these terms explained in simple language, and so for those whose brains have been addled by these terms I think it might help if I gave a short explanation of them, together with the different uses of the muscles and the joints. The average golfer, even if he has heard of them, has only a hazy knowledge of the meaning of flexion and extension, abduction and adduction.

Visualize a man standing with his arms hanging and the palms of his hands forwards. His hands are then in a position of *supination*. He rotates them so that the thumb swings round towards his body; this is *pronation*. His hand moves forwards and this is *flexion*. His hand moves backwards, this is *extension*. Whilst his hand is supinated, if he moves his wrist so that his hand moves away from his body, this is *abduction*. If he moves it nearer his body, this is *adduction*. The only movements which occur in the golf swing are those of abduction and adduction, that is, lateral movements, or what Bob Jones calls "the cock of the wrists." It is of vital importance to realize this, as, the more intelligent the golfer is, the more he is likely to think that the *club head* is moved by the *flexion* or the *extension* of his wrists. Watch any average golfer and it will be noticed that his preliminary "waggle" is a movement of flexion and the extension of the *wrist joints,* while on the other hand the "waggle" of a first class golfer consists of a rocking movement from one foot to the other, and any wrist movement that occurs is one of *abduction* and *adduction*.

Walter Hagen is a marked example of this, and the movements of abduction and adduction of his wrists are exceptionally exuberant. It is also of importance that the golfer should have an elementary knowledge of the action of the muscles that provide the power to propel the club head.

Every joint is moved by at least two opposing sets of muscles: hinged joints that flex and extend the limb, and ball and socket joints that rotate the limb in one direction or another. The power that moves the limb is a nerve impulse, like an electric shock which causes a contraction of the muscles attached to the bones bordering the joint. The stronger the nerve impulse the more violent will be the contraction of the muscles. It is clear that if the opposing muscles contract together equally there will be no movement of the joint, so that to get the greatest amount of power the opposing sets of muscles should be in a state of *complete relaxation*.

Every golfer has had demonstrations of the truth of this, and knows that the length of his drive has little relation to the amount of force which he puts into his shot. In fact, it not infrequently happens that when he takes things easily he will get a longer drive than usual.

The best drives appear to be effortless, and this is due to the opposing muscles not fighting against each other. If a golfer grasps these simple physiological principles thor-

Walter Hagen—one of the best players of the day.

oughly, it will help him to avoid the most grievous of all golfing faults, which is tightening up.

The beginner is always tense, and it takes him many weeks
of practice to learn to relax. Even then, in an emergency, a
feeling of tension is liable to bring about his downfall.

There are few of even the best players who, like Walter
Hagen, can relax more and more according to the greatness
of the occasion. I have watched Walter Hagen play his final
round in five British Open Championships. He is not normally an exceptionally long driver, but I have always been
amazed to see him become not only longer but straighter
when he is in a tight corner, and this appears to be due
entirely to his ability to relax more and more according to
the difficulties against which he has to contend. I think his
most dramatic final rounds were on the occasions when he
knew he had to make certain figures to tie or win. I have a
vivid recollection of seeing him play the difficult finishing
holes at Hoylake when he knew he had to make a series of
fours to tie, and he actually finished one under.

I also remember him playing the last hole at Troon
before twenty thousand spectators, when he had to get a
three to tie with Havers. He played a magnificent drive, and
then a fine iron shot from a bad lie, which hit a small bump
in front of the green and slid into a bunker on the right. If he
had hit a foot to the left he would probably have "laid dead."
Croome, who was referee, said, "Bad luck," but Hagen, who
is a sportsman, replied, "It was not bad luck. I sliced it," and
he then made a gallant effort to hole it out of the bunker.

Even more dramatic was his finish at Lytham and St.
Annes when he had to get two threes at long par four holes
to tie with Bobby Jones. At the 17th he played two excellent
shots, but was still thirty feet from the pin. He took several
minutes to study his putt, and then it remained hanging on
the edge but failed to go in. This left him with a two at the
last hole in order to tie. He played a long straight drive, thirty yards further than I had seen any other competitor, but he
still had a hundred and seventy yards to go. He sent the referee forward to take out the flag, and he then played a high

mashie pitch which dropped within an inch of the cup but ran about fifteen feet beyond it.

It was characteristic of Hagen that, having failed to tie, nothing else mattered so he played carelessly and took four more to hole out.

Great as is the importance of swinging the club head, and although there is a certain degree of truth in Ernest Jones' illustration of a small boy throwing a stone, yet I am convinced that additional help is gained, particularly in those who have started golf late in life, by a clear conception of the swing itself.

I have just been reading some lectures on public speaking by my stepson George Marston Haddock which he is giv-

G. Marston Haddock, President of the College of Music, Leeds, England, MacKenzie's stepson.

ing at Stanford University, and I note that he attaches the utmost importance to teaching how to breathe and devotes a considerable amount of space to the mechanics of breathing. Breathing is the one thing above all others which one would expect to come naturally, and yet it appears that to speak or sing well the majority of people have to be taught. Similarly, doubtless there are many golfers who have learned to swing naturally in their youth, but most of us have to learn how to swing the club head.

I believe one of the reasons that Ernest Jones is so insistent that his pupils should be taught nothing except to swing the club head is that he has realized the harm that had been done in the past by teaching wrong principles. Slow motion pictures have proved that all the old books on golf have not only been useless but harmful, and it is therefore much better to have no theories at all than those that do definite harm.

I have delayed giving my own theories until I was convinced that they were sound, and would be helpful, so I now venture to write my own views on the subject.

It is the club head with which one hits the ball, and so the more rapidly the club head travels, the further the ball will go. The club head may be considered to be set in motion by a series of levers, firmly joined together, forming one composite whole. It is obvious that the further away from the club head the power is applied the more rapidly will the head move.

The lower down the shaft the club is gripped the more slowly will it travel, and if one were to grip it within an inch or so of the head, however much effort one put into it we should be unable to get it to move at any pace at all.

It is obvious, then, that if the shaft of the club, the arms, the body and the legs be considered one composite whole, it is clear that the nearer the feet the power is applied the more rapidly the end of the lever, that is, the club head, will travel.

It is true that the further away the power is applied from the outer edge the greater is the amount of force required to set the club head in motion, but it is here that the most powerful muscles lie, as the muscles of the back, hips and legs are far bigger and more powerful than those of the fingers, wrists and arms.

It is of the utmost importance that one should grasp these fundamental principles. The more highly educated the man, the more likely he is to have a wrong conception of the subject. A boy would try instinctively to bring the larger muscles of his legs and body into play, whereas a man who thinks is more likely to argue that the club is moved by his hands.

I speak feelingly on the subject, as for over thirty years my ideas *have been entirely wrong.*

In the old days at St. Andrews caddies often referred to short approach shots as knee shots. This expression always aroused my derision, and I often remarked that it was perfectly ridiculous to suggest that a club should be moved by one's knees. Nevertheless, I was wrong and they were right.

At the commencement of the backward swing of all good golfers there is a distinct knuckling in of the left knee, but the left heel is not raised. This does not begin until a later period in the swing. The first principle in obtaining the greatest amount of speed in the club head is *to use those muscles that give it the greatest amount of power.* The second principle is to swing the club head in the greatest possible track it will go.

It is obvious that any moving body, such as a motor car, must travel a certain amount of space to attain its greatest degree of momentum, so that the further the club head travels, particularly in a line parallel with the ground, the more rapidly it will be traveling when it comes in contact with the ball.

The path taken by the club head in the backward swing approximates closely, although it is rarely identical with, that taken on the downward swing. Therefore, the longer the path taken by the club going back, the longer and straighter the path it is likely to travel on its return journey.

It is remarkable the distance some of these long drivers like Gene Sarazen can swing their club head back of the ball. If you should watch Gene Sarazen closely, his left shoulder almost appears to be pulled out of its socket.

USGA

Gene Sarazen on the first tee at St. Andrews.

It is important that this should not be confused with a full swing. A so-called full swing is largely an up-and-down movement, and this in itself will not give much length of drive. It is the distance the club is taken back of the ball which counts. There are many long drivers, such as Major Hezlett of the British Walker Cup Team, who get a remarkably long distance with a so-called half swing. On the backswing his club is hardly raised above the shoulder, but he swings his club head back and almost parallel with the ground an exceptionally long distance.

It is important that you should not obtain a wrong mental picture of this and imagine that the club is taken from the ball parallel with the ground in a continuous straight line. The best players, such as Joyce Wethered, take it back straight for a considerable distance, and incidentally forward through the ball for a still greater distance, but as the body rotates *the club head must of necessity conform to the movement of the body and rotate also.* Some of the most stylish players, however, like Harry Vardon for instance, rotate surprisingly little, and can swing with the lower part of their back against a wall without touching it with the club on their back or their forward swing.

I have discussed at some length the anatomical, physiological and mechanical principles of the golf swing because I feel it is important that one should have a clear mental picture as to how the power is applied to move the club head as rapidly as possible.

If man were not a thinking animal, Ernest Jones' teachings would be ideal, and all that would be necessary to obtain a perfect swing would be to imagine the club head is a weight at the end of a string and that you were attempting to swing the weight in the largest arc of a circle that it would go. The powerful muscles I have described would then come into play naturally but, unfortunately, or perhaps I should say fortunately, most men of intelligence cannot repress their thinking powers, and are certain to theorize, so that it is of paramount importance that their theories should be sound.

I am convinced that the theories I have put down are entirely sound. Yesterday, after writing them, I went out to play golf with them firmly planted in my mind. Time after time I outdrove, much to their astonishment, two young fellows who in the past had left me far behind.

Notwithstanding a broken bone in my wrist, and in consequence a wasted left arm, I was driving with deadly accuracy and frequency well over two hundred and thirty yards, and my approach play was equally good, despite the fact I was only playing with four clubs. Although my putting was off, I never played a better round. In the hope that I have made myself clear as to the general principles, I will try and give my conception of the golf swing itself.

In the first place, the grip is of paramount importance. The grip is the connecting link between the body and the club, and if it were to fail no amount of power could possibly be transferred to the club head.

Whatever form of grip is adopted, it is important that it should never vary, as any variation means that the swing would have to be altered to conform with the change of grip.

There are many good players who have different styles of grip, but the important thing to remember is that having once adopted a grip that is comfortable and conforms to any anatomical peculiarities of the hands of the individual, it should never vary. I believe, personally, that the overlapping grip, similar to that of Harry Vardon or of Bob Jones, is the most suitable for most people, although there have been many good players whose grip was entirely different. John Ball, for example, who was the best player of his day, instead of having his right hand, like Harry Vardon, in a position of extreme pronation, kept the palm of his hand well below the shaft of his club. The important thing was, however, that his grip never varied and his swing conformed to it.

Both hands should grip the club firmly, and their relative position should never be changed during any part of the swing. I believe one of the reasons the overlapping grip is the most satisfactory is that if both hands are pronated as far as is comfortable—that is, as much of the knuckles of both hands showing as possible—when the club is gripped you have something very tangible and definite to guide you, and there is no reason why one's grip should ever vary.

It is unnecessary for me to describe in detail the overlapping grip, as every book on golf describes it, and one rarely picks up a golfing paper that has not got at least one illustration of the grip of one or other of the leading players.

The important thing to remember is that both hands must be pronated as far as is comfortable, and it is of vital importance to grip firmly with the left hand and particularly the little finger and ring fingers of the left hand. The importance of this has been brought home to me because the pain caused by the broken bone in my left wrist makes me extremely liable to relax my grip, and on many occasions when I have been clean off my game onlookers have told me that I was letting go with my left hand. It was not until I determined to conquer this fault that there was any marked improvement in my game.

It often seems to me that one of the most difficult things in golf is to grip firmly with one set of muscles at the top of the swing and yet have all one's other muscles in an extreme degree of relaxation.

The grip is of supreme importance. There is a story of Andrew Kirkaldy, who, when he was playing an exhibition match and the President of the club asked him if he would like to wash his hands, replied, "What? Wash ma hands and spoil ma grip?"

❧ *Stance* ❧

One cannot lay down any dogmatic views regarding stance. There are good players with narrow, wide, open, square or closed stances, but here again the important thing is that *the stance should never vary except for a specific purpose,* such as to obtain a voluntary slice or to neutralize the effect of uneven ground.

The majority of the best players have either a square

stance or the right foot very slightly behind the left, and they stand with the ball opposite the left heel.

I believe it is easier to swing smoothly and in the same even path if one stands with the feet fairly close together like Bob Jones. The shorter the shot, the closer the feet should be. The toes should not be pointed too much outwards. They should be almost square, and both knees should be slightly bent and relaxed. The left arm should hang easily but at full stretch. There are many golfers who have their left arm decidedly bent, but it is always a mystery to me that they should be able to get any length or accuracy, as the left arm must straighten on the backward swing, so that the club head is shifting about from one path to another, and one could hardly expect as good results as if it were moving in one smooth even path the whole time.

The preliminary waggle is of importance, as it enables the player to get the feel of the club head. It should consist, as I have already said, of a rocking movement from one foot to the other, and never of flexion, extension, or rotation of the wrists because, as has already been explained, these movements do not occur in the golf swing, and if they are done in the "waggle" nothing but harm can come of it.

The next movement that occurs is the placing of the club head behind the ball. This must be done at right angles to the direction we wish the ball to travel, otherwise one can hardly expect a straight ball to result.

The club head should be taken back forcibly with a certain amount of abandon to overcome its inertia and to start it swinging. The slogan "slow back" is somewhat misleading, as it should be taken back swiftly but *smoothly,* reaching its greatest speed as it is halfway up, and then it should slow down to nothing, *similar to that movement of a pendulum.* At the top of the swing one should relax so completely and slow up to such an extent that you almost feel as if you were going to sleep and to not waken up again until the club head is almost on the ball. The club, however, should never stop completely; it should always be in motion.

The average golfer does exactly the opposite to this. He

The strong, graceful swing of Bobby Jones.

starts painfully slowly then finishes his backswing with a jerk. The excellence of a man's approach play, in particular, can almost be gauged by his exceeding slowness at the top of the swing, but on the other hand his club head never stops moving altogether. I have already said that the club head should be taken back nearly parallel with the ground for as great a distance as possible. This is done by a smooth even pressure downwards and backwards—not downwards and forwards, as this is fatal—of the left shoulder, accompanied by a slight knuckling in (not forwards) of the left knee. This pressure of

224

the left shoulder downwards and backwards is transferred through the arm to the palm of the left hand, which then starts the club head in motion. The head of the club should remain at right angles to the ball for the greatest possible period.

This means that there is no pronation of the left wrist. If there is any rotation at all it should be in the opposite direction, or in other words the little finger and not the index finger of the left hand should be leading in the backward swing.

The late Walter Travis, who, in his day, was the best of all approach players, had a marked supination—that is, rotation anti-clockwise—of his left wrist at the commencement of the swing. There has been much written and spoken of late of the projection of the right hip at the commencement of the backswing. This always seems to me to be putting the cart before the horse, as it is the pressure downward and backwards of the left shoulder which causes the hip to project.

I think perhaps this pressure down and not round of the left shoulder, with the accompanying projection back of the right hip, is the most important thing of all in the swing of the golf club, as if the backswing starts correctly it will have a natural tendency to continue correctly.

Harry Vardon was the first and the greatest exponent of commencing the backswing with a marked downward movement of his left shoulder, and he was by far the most consistent player of his day. This movement causes the weight of the body to be transferred from the left to the right leg. It also creates a straightening of the right knee, thus preventing swaying. We might put this in another way: the whole of the body should not sway, but there should be a considerable amount of sway of the hips, while the right foot and head remain still.

There is an old friend of mine, Colonel Quill, whose battalion I trained in camouflage during the war, who became a scratch-man at sixty years of age after playing golf for only two years. He was an able soldier and sportsman, and took up golf with almost as much enthusiasm as he commanded his battalion.

I have a very vivid recollection of how heartbroken he was on the eve of the departure of his battalion when it was ordered to France and the war office prohibited his going with them because of old age.

He was more virile than many men of half his age and is so still. I met him again last year watching, with the greatest enthusiasm, Sarazen winning the British Open at Sandwich. With the object of keeping his head still, he invented a machine called the Quill-Vardon device, which consisted of a hook, a string and an upright rod with a bell at the top of it. The hook was attached to his cap and the string was threaded through rings on the rod and fastened to the bell at the top, so that whenever he moved his head the bell rang. I do not think that the device was of much value, but he had another contraption which not only prevented him slicing but which enabled him to develop a swing of a similar type to Harry Vardon's.

He attached a long string of rubber between two posts and then practiced the golf swing with the back of his legs touching the rubber band behind him. If he drew his club across the ball, the rubber band caught it on its forward swing. This device taught him to keep his club traveling in a straight line for the longest possible space both before and after it reached the ball. As a substitute for this, swinging with one's back against a wall helps to develop a similar style to Vardon's. To enable one to play accurate golf it is essential that there should be a *fixed pivot* round which the body may swing. *The right leg is this fixed pivot,* and it always seems absurd to me to talk of the head as being this pivot.

Beldam pointed out years ago that slow motion pictures prove that in the case of a good player the club head remains behind the left wrist at the commencement of the backswing. This is due to the downward pressure of the left shoulder being transferred to the left forearm, which bulges backwards creating a hyperextension of the left wrist. The left wrist remains in this state of hyperextension during the whole period of the backswing.

It is very important to realize this because, as has been

pointed out before, almost every man of intelligence has the preconceived impression that the left wrist becomes bent.

I attach a considerable amount of weight to the necessity of starting the swing correctly, as if one obtains a clear mental picture of this the rest of the swing will take care of itself. I watched Bob Jones in his new series of motion pictures at Hollywood, and these pictures show with remarkable clearness every detail of his swing.

They show that in the backswing the club head, owing to the downward movement of the left shoulder, moves for a considerable distance in a direct line back of the ball, and then when the shoulder finally rotates, the club head rotates in conformity with it until the club head points directly backwards. At this point the arm is raised, then the wrists are cocked (abducted), and the backward swing is completed with the toe of the club pointing directly downwards.

Bob Jones shows these different movements in stages, but in the actual swing it is, of course, one continuous movement—smooth and even without the suspicion of a break.

I may say, incidentally, that the initial backward movement in his swing, although firm, is not so forcible as it is in many other good players. But then his whole swing is much slower and easier than that of most champion golfers.

     ❧ There was a remark overheard in the locker room when Bob Jones was changing after a round of golf and a foursome came in, one of whom looked somewhat disheartened. He saw Bob and said, "It is all very well for you to go round a course in the sixties with a swing like yours. I don't consider there is any credit due to you at all. You try and do it with a swing like mine and see what happens." ❧

The unhurried perfection of Bob Jones' swing enables him to get his whole hundred and seventy pounds of weight behind the club head, and he rarely, if ever, makes the almost universal mistake of allowing his weight to get in front of the club. If there is a hundred and seventy pounds at a high rate of speed coming in contact with the ball, something is bound to happen.

There are few, if any, teachers of golf who lay sufficient emphasis on the importance of the whole weight of the body being part and parcel of the club head, but this is clearly as important as the speed the club head is traveling, for the greater the weight behind the club head, the less likely is the speed to be diminished when the club comes in contact with the obstruction of the ball.

The most important thing of all in the golf swing is to feel that it is being executed in such a way that the whole weight of the body will be behind the club head when it comes against the ball, and this is the reason why the finish of the backswing should be unhurried.

Hurrying the finish, or as Bob Jones expresses it, not completing the cock of the wrists, is a fault to which even the best players are liable. The only occasion I ever saw Joyce Wethered off her game was at Wentworth in the international match against America, and this was entirely due to the fact that she was not completing her backswing and was thus failing to get the whole weight of her body behind the club head.

The real meaning of timing is swinging so that the weight is behind and not in front of the club head. Pressing means the opposite.

It is impossible to lay too much stress on the importance of slowing up at the finish of the backswing, but the club should always be in motion and never completely stop.

Slow motion pictures show that Bob Jones and other good players have a slight loop at the top of the swing so that the downward swing of the club is from within outwards, but most players are entirely unconscious of this and an attempt to get it is likely to lead to exaggeration. It occurs naturally in attempting to swing from within out, and is a certain cure for a slice. If it is overdone it results in a pull.

If the backward swing is correct, the forward swing will almost certainly take care of itself.

In the backswing the left hand is in control, but in the

forward swing there is a gradually increasing pressure of the right hand, and the club head should follow through parallel with the ground for the longest possible space.

One hears a great deal of the importance of a straight left arm, but I believe that an attempt to straighten the left arm at the top of the swing will only lead to rigidity, whereas on the other hand swinging the club back of the ball as far as possible will straighten the left arm, and a straight left arm is an indication that one has done so. Similarly, a straight right arm is an indication that the player has followed through correctly.

A man of intelligence will naturally wish to know what possible influence the follow-through can have on the flight of the ball, and will say, "What can it matter what happens after the ball is struck?"

A complete follow-through, however, is an indication that the club head has been traveling at its greatest pace when it comes in contact with the ball, and moreover it is not generally known that the club head remains in contact with the ball for quite an appreciable time, and this is so to such an extent that the ball is actually flattened when the club connects with it. Many golfers, after hitting a new ball, may have noticed the surprisingly large impression made by the paint on the face of a wooden club.

If the follow-through is restricted, it means that a distinct check has been put on the pace of the club head before it reaches the ball.

When Johnnie de Forest was asked at the San Francisco Chamber of Commerce luncheon to tell how he managed to win the British Amateur Championship, he stated that for some weeks previously his golf had been terrible, he could hardly break ninety on any golf course, and then on the eve of the Championship he went to see one of Bob Jones' movie pictures and while watching it he suddenly realized that his own hip movements were not correct, so he determined during every shot in the Championship that he would swing so that his *right hip pointed towards the hole*. These were not his exact words, but then Johnnie has a gift of

Joyce Wethered. Observe her right hip.

expressing himself in a far more lucid and entertaining way than I can hope to compete with.

The pointing of the right hip towards the hole in the follow-through is of special importance in short approach shots and in bunker shots. It makes bunker play so simple that it is almost as easy to approach accurately from a bunker as from a good lie. It is an indication that the club head is traveling parallel with the ground for the longest possible period.

Joyce Wethered is, I think, the most consistently accurate approach player of all first class golfers. Observe her balance in a photograph of the finish of an approach shot. Her right hip has come through in a remarkable manner and she is poised with the ease and grace of a perfect dancer. On the other hand, the average golfer's swing is a down and up movement, and the club head does not travel parallel with the ground for a longer period than that of a pendulum.

To obtain a perfect follow-through, the fulcrum as well as the head of the pendulum must be in motion.

Approaching in the way I have described gives a much greater security against error, as one is not so dependent on an accurate eye.

I may say here, incidentally, that the best players, like Bob Jones, *rarely under club themselves,* but on the other hand they never omit a complete follow-through. If they wish to spare a shot they take a shorter grip and follow-through to the fullest possible extent.

In my conception of the golf swing I have said little about keeping one's eye on the ball and the many slogans that are being constantly drummed into the unfortunate golfer. *Keeping the eye on the ball is of secondary importance,* as if the swing is correctly executed the club head will return naturally to the spot from which it started.

It is true that it is not only essential to keep your eye on the ball, *but on one spot on the ball,* and to continue to keep one's eye in the same position for an appreciable period of time after the ball has started its flight; but too great a concentration, as if one were hypnotized, has the effect of causing a down and up movement instead of a perfect follow-through.

Too great concentration on keeping the head still or keeping the chin pointed towards the right has similar disadvantages. Keeping the chin pointed too much towards the right, as advocated by Alec Morrison, has also the disadvantage of the bridge of the nose obstructing the sight of the right eye and thus depriving us of bifocal vision.

Anyone can test the truth of this by turning the chin to the right and then closing the left eye, and he will then find that the ball has disappeared from view.

As I am writing this on my porch facing the 6th fairway of Pasatiempo, I see a player approaching the green. He has his chin pointing in a most marked manner to the right and has fluffed his shot. He drops another and another with similar results. This is entirely due to too rigid concentration causing a down and up movement and preventing a true follow-through. One can see the same thing happen any day on any golf course. A striking tribute to Alec Morrison's writings and personality—nevertheless, in this respect, I think that he is wrong.

Keeping the head still, the chin fixed in one position or even too great a concentration of the eye on the ball is only too apt to lead to tension and rigidity. Yet again if one keeps the eye glued on the ball from the address onwards, it is likely to tire one to such an extent that the concentration is lost at the time when it really matters, namely when the club head is reaching the ball.

At the time the club is *just about to hit the ball,* not only is it desirable to keep the eye on the ball, but on one spot on the ball.

There are many other points regarding the golf swing which might be clarified. We have already stated that the swing pivots round the right leg. During the address the right knee should be kept slightly bent and relaxed. One of the most fatal mistakes of the beginner is rising on the right leg. The leg straightens itself naturally without any voluntary effort if the club is taken back correctly. It is important that

MacKenzie on his porch overlooking the 6th fairway at Pasatiempo.

the pivot, that is, the right leg, should be relaxed and still, as otherwise it is impossible to swing smoothly in one even groove, and inaccuracy is assured.

One cannot emphasize too strongly that the club head must travel through parallel with the ground. The most grievous fault of the beginner is attempting to pick up the ball. He does not realize that it is the loft of the club face that raises the ball in the air. The more highly educated the novice is, the more is he likely to imagine that it requires some voluntary effort to raise the ball, whereas lifting the club head as it reaches the ball is certain to top it.

My wife and daughter-in-law have just commenced to play golf. At first, being thinking and intelligent people, they constantly topped the ball time after time owing to their subconscious efforts to loft it. On the other hand, my

233

daughter-in-law's boy, a little fellow of four years old, raises it in the air with a baby wooden club every time.

The old adage "a little knowledge is a dangerous thing" is as applicable to the golf swing as anything else. We should either have no knowledge at all or should study the subject so thoroughly that it becomes second nature.

The faults of the beginner—such as topping, slicing, pulling and all the other pitfalls into which one has fallen, and many of the misconceptions written recently about hitting the ball from within out—might have been avoided if the golfing public realized the mechanics of the spin of the golf ball.

Professor Tait, the father of Freddie Tait, wrote a great deal about this in the days of the guttie ball. He wrote an

MacKenzie with his stepgrandson, Phil Haddock at Pasatiempo.

article to prove that no human being, however powerful, could propel a golf ball more than a certain distance. Then his own son went out and hit a ball several yards further than his father had considered possible. This gave Professor Tait much food for thought, and he began to make fresh investigations of the subject and came to the conclusion that the added flight of a golf ball was due to its spin, which enabled it to fight against the effects of gravity.

A well struck ball is hit from above downwards, and this results in backspin which, owing to the friction of the air, enables it to climb. The observant will notice that a well-hit ball flies straight and at the end of its flight begins to rise. On the other hand, a badly hit ball struck with an ascending club at the end of flight ducks.

In the early days of the guttie it was noticed that a ball which had been hacked with a club flew further than one which was smooth. This was due to the friction of the air

Hilda Sykes Haddock MacKenzie.

235

influencing the spine of a rough ball and causing it to rise more readily than a smooth one. The balls were then hammered to make them rough so as to get a similar effect to a ball that had been hacked with a club.

It may help us to understand more readily the effects of the spin of a golf ball if we compare it to a billiard ball. A billiard ball hit below the centre tends to rise, but if it is hit above, its tendency is to hug the cloth.

Similarly, if a golf ball has underspin, the friction of the air is greater on the under surface and it therefore tends to rise over the obstruction of the air. On the other hand, if a ball has topspin, the friction of the air is greatest on the upper surface and it tends to duck below the obstruction.

If a ball has a pulled or a sliced spin, the friction of the air has a similar effect.

A ball struck from within out causes a similar spin to that of a billiard ball hit on the right-hand side: the friction of the air is therefore greater on the right-hand side, so that the ball curves from right to left. On the other hand, a ball struck from without in spins in the opposite direction and is sliced.

Bob Jones, in a recent article on swinging from within out, points out that every first class golfer can swing within out or from without in at will, and that there are occasions when it may be desirable to do either the one or the other.

Harold Hilton many years ago wrote a chapter in Mr. John L. Low's book *Concerning Golf,* in which he describes how to make use of the wind. He says that when the wind is blowing from the right to left *he plays into it with a pull* so that the ball at the end of its flight gets the help of the wind, and on the contrary if the wind is blowing from left to right *he plays into it with a slice* so that it again gets the help of the wind at the end of its flight.

A controlled spin was of far greater importance in the days of the guttie or the Haskell than it is with the small heavy ball of today which is not so easily influenced by the wind. If, as many of us hope, we shall return to the floater, the pleasure of making shots of this description will be restored to golf.

If the average golfer considers carefully what I have written on the spin of the golf ball and the swing of the club head, he cannot fail to improve his game.

Slicing, as we have stated, is caused by hitting the ball from without in. It may be corrected and even converted into a pull by hitting the ball from within out, and the easiest way to do this is to get the mental picture of throwing the club head through the ball, outwards and parallel with the ground.

If one always swings in the same groove as one ought to, the easiest way of obtaining a voluntary slice is to address the ball with the right foot slightly more forward than normal, and conversely if a pull is desired the right foot should be placed further back. There are one or two other points which we might discuss: socketing (shanking), for instance, is a plague that ruins the games of even the best players. J. H. Taylor suffered from it for two years.

Immediately after the war I saw the final of the Army Championship, which in 1919 took the place of the British Amateur Championship, between Lord Charles Hope and Lister Kaye. Lister Kaye was, if I remember rightly, dormie seven when he shanked a shot and lost a hole. I remarked to a friend who was with me that the fear of shanking was its greatest cause. I wouldn't be surprised if he continues to shank and then Charles Hope may have a chance. He did continue to do so and Lord Charles Hope beat him at the 37th hole. Lister Kaye never recovered from his fear of shanking, and ten years afterwards his handicap had gone up from scratch to 12.

For twenty years I have been an habitual shanker. On scores of occasions in a tight match I have said to myself the only thing that could possibly prevent my winning this match is to shank, and by gosh I have done so.

Shanking is due to overanxiety causing a hurry of the finish of the backswing so that the whole weight of the body is on the toes, and instead of being behind, the club head starts down in front of it and then the ball is hit with the shank of the club, causing it to shoot off at right angles.

Today not even the fear of shanking causes me to do so. I have apparently been entirely cured by determining to complete the cock of the wrists before commencing the downward swing.

Beginners rarely shank, as they are habitually over-swingers in short approach shots.

Keeping the eye on the ball and the maxim of "slow back" are no remedy for shanking. In fact, they make it worse.

Quick back, then slow, and a determination to complete the backswing smoothly and easily without any stoppage at the top are the only certain cures.

One or two points regarding mashie and niblick play might be discussed with advantage.

Always grip the club firmly and even forcibly with both hands. One of the difficulties in golf is to grip fiercely and yet have all the other muscles in a state of complete relax-ation. J. H. Taylor was perhaps the best "lofter" of his day, or for that matter any other day, and no one ever gripped a mashie more fiercely than he did, yet at the top of his swing all his other muscles were in a state of extreme relaxation.

Every good approacher takes a divot after his ball has been struck. This is due to the club head following through into the ground with the whole weight of the body behind it. On the other hand an indifferent player picks up the ball cleanly because his swing is a down and up movement, and any good result he may attain is entirely due to an accurate eye.

There are a few dandelions on the fairway in front of my house and I practice approach shots with a dandelion in front of the ball, and I know that any shot has not been per-fect unless the whole of that dandelion has been removed.

The same principle applies to bunker shots. The follow-through, with the right hip pointing directly towards the hole, is of paramount importance.

I was watching Mortie Dutra play a most difficult shot out of a footmark in a bunker during the match play cham-pionship at San Francisco. He addressed the ball, waggled his hips, stopped, waggled again, rested an appreciable time, waggled his hips more forcibly than ever and finally swung. His club slowed down beautifully, smoothly at the top of his backswing and then came down on the ball, which finished two inches from the cup.

The difficulty of most golfers with bunker shots is that they think they have an exceptional shot to play and they swing exceptionally badly. *The more difficult the shot, the more smoothly one should swing.*

❈ *The Run Up Shot* ❈

There is one shot that even the best of the American golfers have trouble with, and that is the run up shot. Even the incomparable Bob Jones never learned to play it well until he had played for some time at St. Andrews. One of the reasons for this is that there are few American golf courses where a knowledge of the run up shot is essential. It always seems to me that an inartistic pitch at every hole becomes monotonous. We have tried to rectify this at the Augusta National, and have constructed many of the greens so that when the ground is hard and dry a knowledge of the run up shot is essential.

Most American greens are overwatered, and it is hoped that we will not make this mistake at Augusta.

Many good golfers play a run up shot like a putt with an almost straight faced club, but I, personally, prefer a number five, as I can then pitch the ball a longer or shorter distance according to the undulations between me and the flag.

The run up shot is played with topspin, whereas the pitch is played with underspin. There are not many golfers who can switch from one to the other with the confidence of Joyce Wethered.

The best run up players address the ball opposite their right toe. They take the club back as near the ground as possible and when the club head reaches the ball they turn the right hand over as in locking a door. A very complete follow-through, with the right hip pointing to the hole, is essential. It is not necessary or even desirable to take a divot, because the club head is moving upwards, and not downwards as in a lofting shot.

⚭ *Putting* ⚭

This chapter would be incomplete unless I made some remarks about putting.

A few weeks ago I was in despair. I had a similar nervous jab as that which has ruined Harry Vardon's golf during recent years. I could even tell by the sound of the club on the ball that my putting was all wrong, and yet during the thirty years when the rest of my golf was rotten I was a consistently good putter. Putting is largely a question of confidence, and it is unwise to dogmatize on the subject. The best putter I know is Walter Egan, Chandler Egan's cousin. He putts entirely from the shoulder joints. There are others who putt almost entirely from their wrists and many others use both wrists and shoulders, but they all have one characteristic in common, and that is that the club head is always moving in a straight line between the ball and the hole.

A good way of practicing putting is to lay two clubs parallel on the ground and try to putt between them without touching either on the forward or the backward swing.

I rarely approach and putt well during the same round, and I think that this is due to the fact that I am approaching my best when I am gripping the club very firmly, but on the other hand my putting is never really good unless I am gripping the club lightly in my fingers, and it is difficult without conscious effort to switch over from one grip to another, for unfortunately the best golf is played doing all these things subconsciously.

One of the best tips I know is one given by Bob Jones and that is to keep the left elbow always pointing to the hole.

A change of putter sometimes helps when one is off one's game. I returned recently to an old aluminium putter and this has restored my confidence, and as I said before *confidence is almost everything in putting.* This being so, we will say no more on the subject.

When I started to write this chapter I thought it would be easy, in a few pages, to describe an action like hitting a golf ball which takes less than a second in time, but the more I wrote the more difficult I found it to describe clearly and concisely my views on the subject, and I doubt if I would have ventured to discuss the matter had I not felt that others have written thousands of pages which are not only misleading but harmful. Many of the best golfers have found that when they began teaching or writing their ideas on golf it has had a detrimental effect on their game. In my case, however, it has had exactly the opposite effect, and I have discovered that my golf has continued to improve with every page I wrote. This has convinced me more than ever that what I have written will be helpful to dubs, like I have been until recently, and particularly to professionals and businessmen who are blessed with intelligence and education.

⚜ *A Summary to Score* ⚜

I might summarize my views as follows: It is the head of the club with which one hits the ball. The hands are the connecting link between the powerful muscles of the body and the club. Start the backswing with a down and backwards movement of the left shoulder, which should continue moving back smoothly until the muscles attached to the left shoulder blade are fully stretched. Complete the "cock of the wrist" at the finish of the backswing and relax completely. Start the downswing smoothly, with gradually increasing pressure through the hands, and follow-through parallel

The putting stroke of Bobby Jones.

with the ground as far as the club head will go so that the right hip is pointing to the hole.

If the player attempts to carry out these principles in practice, there will be a greater and greater tendency for them to become subconscious when playing in a match or a medal round. The best golf is played subconsciously, without any attempt to analyze the different movements of the joints that comprise the golf swing.

I have just read what I have written to my wife, who criticizes it by saying, "You should have left out your recapitulation, as you have said the same thing several times already." I may have been somewhat redundant, but as even the art of advertising is repetition, so it is equally essential to reiterate constantly anything which one wishes to bring forcibly home to people.

✳ A friend of mine was Junior Counsel to the eminent British lawyer Lockwood. Lockwood had put up his case for the defense without making any definite impression on the jury, then my friend rose and put up his argument and before sitting down whispered to Lockwood, "Shall I say anything else?" "Say it again," said Lockwood, so he went through his argument again in different words and, having come to an end, once more he asked Lockwood if he should say anything else. "Say it again," repeated Lockwood. So my friend went over his argument again until finally there was a glimmering of intelligence on the face of the jury. The upshot of it was that they won their case. ✳

It was this case that brought home to me the value of the slogan "Say it again." If I have come back too often to the same points in this chapter it is because of the great importance that I attach to them. Having said this, it only remains for me to say to those of you who have not perfected your golf swing, *"Go back to the beginning and read it again."*

Portrait of Dr. Alister MacKenzie.

❈7❈
Some Thoughts on Golf

My friend, Max Behr, has written learnedly and at great length to prove that golf is not a game but a sport. He may be, and probably is, quite right, but it is no good quibbling about words; the chief thing to bear in mind is that golf is a recreation and a means for giving us health and pleasure.

How often have we known committees, presumably consisting of men of intelligence, receiving the statement that golf is played for fun, with eyes and mouths wide open in astonishment? It is always difficult to persuade them that the chief consideration that should influence us in making any alterations to a golf course is to give the greatest pleasure to the greatest number. Any change to a course that does not do this is manifestly a failure.

The only reason for the existence of golf and other games is that they promote the health, pleasure and even the prosperity of the community.

It is surprising how few politicians and others realize the extent that golf courses and other playing fields do this; they appear to think that anything that promotes happiness is an evil and should be taxed out of existence.

I have known even an ardent golfer stating that it was an outrage that a golf course should be constructed on wheat land. He did not appear to realize that there are hundreds of times as much land devoted to wheat as to golf, and that, moreover, wheat can be grown away from the big cities, whereas golf courses for the masses are of value only when they are in close proximity to large towns.

A good golf course is a great asset to a nation.

Those who harangue against land being diverted from agriculture and used for golf have little sense of proportion. Comparing the small amount of land utilized for golf and other playing fields with the large amount devoted to agriculture, we get infinitely more value out of the former than the latter. We all eat too much.

During the Great War, in Britain, the majority were all the better for being rationed and getting a smaller amount of food, but none of us get enough fresh air, pleasurable excitement and exercise.

Health and happiness are everything in this world. Money grubbing, so-called business, except insofar as it helps to attain this, is of minor importance.

One of the reasons why I, a medical man, decided to give up medicine and take to golf architecture was my firm conviction of the extraordinary influence on health of pleasurable excitement, especially when combined with fresh air and exercise. How frequently have I, with great difficulty, persuaded patients who were never off my doorstep to take up golf, and how rarely, if ever, have I seen them in my consulting room again.

❧ I recently came across a lady I had not seen for over twenty years. She said, "I shall always be grateful to you, Dr. MacKenzie, for what you did for me." I replied that I was not aware of doing anything for her. She said, "Oh yes! You did. You persuaded my husband to play golf. Before then he said he had no time for golf, he sat all day and every day in his office, went to church on Sunday, then ate too much and was not fit to live with for the rest of the week. Since he played golf he is not only physically fit but mentally alert.

He has given up grumbling at me and at his office staff, he is a pleasure to live with and his business is infinitely more successful." ✛

Until recent years every man was ashamed of playing golf. He sneaked off from his home or office as though he were committing some crime. The general public looked upon anyone who played golf with the utmost contempt, and considered that, being a golfer, he must be useless at everything else.

It was said that Briand and his ministry owed their downfall after the war to the fact that Briand was discovered having a lesson in putting from Lloyd George.

What is the real truth? Those who rave against golf surely forget that many of the greatest politicians, thinkers and businessmen conserve their health and their mental powers through golf. As examples we could quote some of the greatest minds in the past, such as President Wilson, Carnegie, Lord Northcliffe, A. J. Balfour and Asquith, and today all or almost all the greatest men of the English speaking races owe their mental alertness to golf. Golf does not require the whole day, nor is it essential to make arrangements beforehand. Moreover, it is not too strenuous and can be played up to any age.

There appears to be no sign of any decreased popularity—rather, the reverse. The elusiveness of golf is sufficient to ensure its abiding popularity. No one ever seems to master it. You imagine that you have got the secret, but it is like a bird of passage—here today and gone tomorrow.

This is so in all things which are worthwhile. There are some games, such as roller skating and table tennis, which become merely passing crazes, and this is so because one obtains a certain standard of proficiency which neither increases nor decreases, and in consequence the game becomes monotonous. Golf on a first class course can never become monotonous, and the better the course, the less is it likely to do so. Golf on a good links is, in all probability, the best game in the world. On the late Victorian type of inland course, however, where there is a complete lack of variety, flat fairways, flat unguarded greens, long grass necessitating searching for lost balls, mathematically placed hazards consisting of the cop or pimple variety, which not only offend all the finest instincts of the artist and the sportsman, it becomes the most boring game in existence.

The advent of the golf course architect has largely, though not entirely, cured these disabilities. The majority of amateurs are sportsmen and welcome anything that increases the sporting and dramatic element in the game.

There are some of the best players, however, who look upon golf in the card and pencil spirit, and resent anything which interferes, as they think, with their steady series of threes and fours. I have already mentioned how some of the good players altered some of the sporting features of Moortown which they considered had a destructive effect on their cards, and how the long handicap players, like true sportsmen, insisted that the architect be recalled to restore the course to its original condition.

There was an article by Kolin Robertson, the golf writer, which may have influenced them in their decision. The following is an extract from it:

⚹ "I have in mind a certain golfing hole which, in the past at any rate, constituted the perfect test of golf. I refer to the thirteenth at Moortown. Every stout hearted Moortown player will remember that slantwise-lying catchy little hollow which has now been filled in so that the whole of the green is now practically level with the fairway. How often did that hollow make the golfer approach the green in installments, and how often did it enable the bold spirit and accomplished golfer, taking his fate in his hand, to go for glory and a win. To say the least, the filling in of that hollow has made the approach to that hole simply child's play." ⚹

One of the reasons and possibly the chief reason why, compared with other countries, the boom in golf in Britain is on the wane is that committees are frequently perpetrating the same errors as at Moortown, so that the members lose their interest in golf without knowing the reason why they have done so. One of the difficulties is that new committees, instead of giving credit to the original members who have done all the pioneer work, are often amazingly jealous of them, and, as new members of a committee are often appointed because they are better players, they think they know more about the game, and have a burning desire to put their mark upon the course. They therefore call in some professional who they think will back their views, and then they proceed to make changes. As I stated before, the results are always disastrous. I do not know of a single example of any real improvement having been made in this way. Bitter experience has convinced us so strongly of the folly of making alterations without expert advice that during recent years we have persuaded the founders of most of our golf courses to pass a resolution that no alterations or additions be made to our courses except on the advice of the architect or one of equal eminence.

On every occasion when we have persuaded the directors to make this a condition of the foundation of the club, the course has remained an outstanding success and has continued to increase in popularity year by year.

One of the reasons why golf is an expensive game is that there are far too many people connected with golf who think because they can play golf that they are qualified to advise on golf courses.

There is an old Persian saying:

He who knows not and knows not that he knows not is a fool.
Avoid him.
He who knows not and knows that he knows not will learn.
Teach him.

He who knows and knows not that he knows, will fail.
Pity him.
He who knows and knows that he knows is a wise man.
Follow him.

If more people connected with the promotion and upkeep of golf courses knew that they knew not, the game would probably not cost a quarter as much as at present, and as is the case of motor cars in America, would no longer be considered a luxury but a necessity for the promotion of the health, the happiness and the prosperity of the community.

Today one can almost gauge the intelligence and prosperity of a community by the extent golf and golf courses are booming. In America there is a tremendous boom in golf; in Russia there is none.

With the exception of ignorant politicians who, with a few notable exceptions, appear to desire to tax golf courses and playing fields out of existence, most people know that golf and other games promote the health and happiness of the community, but there are few who realize the extent to which it promotes the prosperity of the world.

Some years ago I was designing a golf course on the East coast of England which was financed by an old man and one who did not play golf. I was curious to know why he, a non-golfer, should finance the club, so one day I asked him.

He said, "During the war twelve of my clerks started to play golf. They became so much more mentally alert and so much more useful to me that I concluded golf was a great asset in promoting the prosperity of the community, and I decided to promote it to the fullest extent in my power."

I hope to live to see the day when there are the crowds of municipal courses, as in Scotland, cropping up all over the world. It would help enormously in increasing the health, the virility and the prosperity of nations, and would do much to counteract discontent and Bolshevism. There can be no possible reason against, and there is every reason in favour of, municipal courses.

They invariably pay, and I have never known one, unlike other municipal ventures, that was a burden on the rates and taxes of the community.

On the other hand, municipal golf courses, like all other municipal undertakings, invariably cost too much, and some of them are appallingly bad. The reason is that municipalities try to economize on expert advice, and even if they employ a good architect they are not prepared to pay enough for expert foremen.

If the cost and upkeep of municipal courses were less, far more people would be able to play golf. It is a well-known economic fact that if you halve the cost of an article the demand is usually increased eightfold.

There is an increasing number of pay-as-you-play courses run as private ventures, but one of the difficulties of these is that it is not as easy for a private individual to get hold of such suitable golfing ground as a municipality, and moreover, when the ground becomes more valuable a private individual is only too likely to sell it for building purposes.

A municipality has no such temptation, as, apart from golf, an open space is always an asset as one of the lungs of the city. Ninety-nine out of a hundred municipal golf courses are constructed from a purely penal point of view, whereas it is more essential that they should be constructed on strategic lines even than private courses.

On municipal courses there should be no rough, a minimum of bunkers, and the interest should consist almost entirely in the character of the undulations. St. Andrews is perfect in this respect. Max Behr's Lakeside course, where Bob Jones made some of his movie pictures, with the exception of two holes, is almost ideal for a municipal course.

The dub can top or slice almost every shot without any dire punishment, and yet Bob Jones says that there is no other inland course where he has to play such accurate golf to do a good score.

Bayside in Long Island will, we hope, be equally good. There are only nineteen bunkers on it and no rough at all.

Municipal golf should never entail the expense of caddies

or of lost balls. If a municipal course is a good one, the regular players take such an intense pride in it that they lessen the cost of upkeep by replacing not only the divots they have removed themselves, but also those left behind by other players, and seeing that everyone else replaces their divots.

I recently visited two municipal courses in Leeds, England, which I had made, and found to my great delight that they were freer from divot marks than any private course. On inquiry I discovered that the members took so much pride in it that they not only replaced their own divots but also any which they found lying about.

❧ *Caddies* ❧

Many of the world's best players have learned their golf at St. Andrews, Carnoustie and other municipal courses, and with a few notable exceptions the remainder have learned their golf as caddies. Twenty years ago I thought, with other people, that the one blot on golf was the caddy system. We thought it was a very bad training for youth, a lazy life, a blind alley occupation. We instituted schemes for educating them, such as training in gardening and other kindred subjects. Since then I have been astonished to find how well caddies do in later life.

On several occasions well dressed men have accosted me and told me that they caddied for me years ago in Leeds or some other place. Some of them were well-to-do tradesmen, commercial travellers, engineers, one a superintendent of police, insurance managers, professional golfers and so on. Few of them would have been content to spend their lives gardening.

I attribute their doing so well in later life to the fact that contact with men of greater education stimulates their ambition, and perhaps, amongst other things, improves their speech.

Caddying is a healthy occupation, so that caddies start their adult life with healthy minds and bodies. Moreover, employers of labour take more interest and are more likely to promote boys who have caddied for them.

Another reason why caddying is excellent training for youth is that there is no game which teaches honesty to the same extent as golf. There is no referee, and the rules are based on the assumption that every golfer is strictly honest. What other game depends on the integrity of the player to such an extent, that even if he is out in the rough, alone with his maker, and loses a stroke because his ball rolls over in addressing it, he must at once acquaint his opponent with the penalty?

I have known many examples of golfers who have got themselves thoroughly disliked because they did not trust their opponents on these occasions.

Caddies are quick to sense any suspicion of dishonesty among players, and there is no player that caddies have so much contempt for as one who has an evil reputation of this kind. Golf, unlike politics, is an honest game.

> ❧ There was a Lord Mayor I knew, an ardent politician, who had the reputation of being a bad counter. On arrival on a green, his opponent asked him how many strokes he had had, and he replied, "five." His opponent said "Oh no! You have taken more than that." The Lord Mayor turned to his caddy and said, "How many strokes have I had?" The caddie replied, "Seven, sir." "You little liar," replied the Mayor, "I've only had six." ❧

An intelligent caddie often knows more about the rules than some of the players. Many of the players are as ignorant of rules as the small boy who wrote in his examination paper that, "A papal bull is a bull kept at the Vatican to give milk to the Pope's children."

❧ *Rules of Golf* ❧

The rules of golf are becoming more complicated and more difficult to remember. Many of us think that it was a great mistake, and contrary to the spirit of golf, that any alteration was made in the original form of match play, that one should play a ball from where it lies or give up the hole. In the old days it was remarkable from what seemingly unplayable positions one managed to extract a ball. Today we lose all the joy in doing so and also the training in playing spectacular shots of this description.

The Royal and Ancient Rules of Golf Committee have given in far too much to the English, Scottish and Irish unions.

In these days there is far too much talk about democracy. The general public are always, or almost always, wrong. We get far sounder judgment from a benevolent autocracy who are thoroughly steeped in the traditions and spirit of the game.

The traditional attitude of the Royal and Ancient Club was: We make these rules for the club. If the rest of the world wish to adopt them, we will help in the interpretation of them to the fullest extent in our power. If on the other hand they do not desire our assistance, let them, as they say in Scotland, "gang their ain gait."

Let us hope that instead of being led by the rest of the world, the Royal and Ancient will return to the spirit that animated them in the days of the greatest sportsman among golfers, the late John L. Low.

It is a very fortunate thing for golf that most of the committee of the United States Golf Association today, and in the past, has consisted of men who realize that golf is a game and that it is essential that the sporting spirit of the game should not be destroyed.

It would have been so easy for them in the attempt to make golf strictly equitable to destroy all its thrills, and in the long run make it infinitely more unfair than it was before. Today the average American golf course is more sporting than the average British one, but I still think that the best British courses are superior to those in America.

There are some who have suggested that the superiority of the American golfers over the British might have been due to the excellence of the American courses. I do not believe such to be the case. I think that the chief reason for the United States' superiority is that Americans take the game far more seriously than the British.

Nearly every American takes his score, a Briton rarely does so.

Americans practice much more assiduously. If he is "off his game" with any club, he takes that club out and practices until he gets "on" again.

In Britain the women take golf much more seriously than the men. They are also constantly practicing and rarely play a round without taking their "score." The consequence is that they can more than hold their own with American women.

I think there is every excuse for British amateurs not taking the game too seriously, but there is no excuse for British professionals. It is their business to play golf, yet they rarely practice. I have attended most of the British Championships for the last twenty years, and it is always the Americans that one sees out on the course practicing in the evening.

I was lunching with John Ball at Hoylake a few years ago, and he remarked that if you looked out of the clubhouse window almost any evening twenty years ago you would see three figures silhouetted against the skyline swinging clubs. The three figures were Harold Hilton, Jack Graham and himself, and that was the reason they enjoyed such marked superiority over other golfers. I am not suggesting that British amateurs should take the game as seriously as British women and Americans. On the contrary, I believe that the British attitude is the right one, and that they get far more health and happiness out of the game than their own womenfolk or the Americans.

❈ *Match vs. Medal* ❈

I believe that one gets far more fun in playing a match for five or ten dollars and licking one's opponent by lofting a stymie on the last green than you can ever get in taking your score. If your score is a good one you will remember it, but if it is a bad one why make life a burden by doing so?

In Scotland, on completing a round, no one ever asked you "What is your score?" It is always, "Did you beat him?" or "Was it a tight match?"

At some clubs in England and in a small minority in America the question is the same as it is in Scotland, but on many courses in England and on most in America it is, "What is your score?" or "What did you shoot?"

In Britain, the better the course the greater the match and the less the medal play.

It often seems to me that on a good course golfers get their fun in attempting the varied and thrilling shots that are required and in trying to beat their opponents, but on an indifferent course the only excitement they get is their score. Surely there is far more fun in a contest against flesh and blood than against a card and pencil.

There is nothing that worries me so much as playing against a man who thinks only of his card and is perfectly indifferent to yours, unless it is perhaps playing with one who is over- sympathetic about your bad luck and your misfortunes.

I once played with an ex-champion who always religiously took his score. I started to play the game of my life, whereas he was not doing too well. At the first hole I holed an approach for three, at the second I got a long putt for a two, at the third a three and at the fourth—a par five—a four. On the fifth tee he turned to me and said, "Aren't WE playing tripe?"

I like to play against a sportsman who never grouses about his own bad luck, is unstinting in praise where praise is due, but at the same time is sufficiently human to take an unholy joy in your misfortunes. There is some fun in beating an opponent of that type.

I think it was Wellington whose advice was asked by a mother as to the suitability of a man for a husband of her daughter. Wellington advised her to invite him to breakfast. Today you would invite him to golf.

Recently my wife asked me my opinion of a man who was managing certain of her affairs, and I told her I would ask him to play golf with me.

I lent him some clubs. He was apparently a good player, but it was obvious that the clubs did not suit him, and I got several holes from him. He never groused about the clubs or the course, but played a gallant uphill fight and finally finished, to his great delight, in getting a two at a par four hole. I was able to confirm my wife's opinion that he was a sportsman and that she could have every confidence in him.

There are many of us who firmly believe that a contest between flesh and blood is the only true form of golf, and that too much attention to score play is detrimental to the real interest of the game.

If too much attention were paid to the vitriolic outbursts of unsuccessful competitors in medal rounds, there would not be a first class hole left in golf.

It is always the hole that gives the most lasting pleasure and excitement, like the Road and Eden Holes at St. Andrews, which are most fiercely criticized.

Golfers must have something to talk about, and they usually talk most about something they imagined spoilt their score. They rarely attribute their misfortune to the real cause, and that is that they have not played their shots quite well enough. Amongst other thoughts on golf, one's mind turns to putting.

⚔ *Making Putting Easier* ⚔

There are vandals in Britain who have failed to grasp the tradition and spirit of the game to such an extent that they would enlarge the holes in the putting greens. Gene Sarazen has advocated similar ideas.

There are others in America who advocate that only half

a stroke should be counted for each putt. In other words, if a player takes four putts on a green it should only be counted as two strokes.

Even if it were desirable to give players still further advantages for brute force as compared with finesse and skill, consider the complications to which such a ruling is going to lead. The putting green is defined, according to the rules of golf, as "that area, excepting hazards, within twenty yards of the hole." Would players be expected to carry measuring tapes so as to define accurately the margins of the putting greens? The advocates of these innovations suggest that the area of the putting green can be readily defined by the closely mown surface, but it has often been pointed out that on first class golf courses there should be no defined margin between the approach and the putting green.

Indeed, on golf courses like St. Andrews in Scotland there is no margin, and players frequently use their putters up to fifty yards, or more, away from the hole.

A man's skill or finesse in approaching and putting should not be neutralized in this way. A man who approaches so accurately that he can get down in one putt deserves to be adequately rewarded.

I remember once seeing Brownlow, a frail and delicate man, but a most skillful player, squaring a match in the semi-final of the British Amateur Championship at Muirfield when he was playing, I think, against Jesse Sweetzer, by getting down in one putt on the 16th, 17th, and 18th greens. Why should even the spectators be deprived of thrills of this description? One of the greatest delights and greatest thrills in golf is beating an opponent who is three up and only four of five to go and our only hope is sinking one or two spectacular putts. Why should all hope of doing this sort of thing be taken away from us?

In order to arrive at a decision as to the right or wrong of any social or economic problem, one should always be guided by the lessons of history. One has only to imagine what would have been the effect on the popularity of golf if innovations of this kind had been introduced thirty years ago, pandering still more to brute force as opposed to finesse and skill. There were two incidents in the history of the game which did more to put golf on the front page of the newspapers and increase its popularity in America than anything else. One was the winning of the British Amateur Championship by Walter Travis, and the other was the defeat of Harry Vardon and Ted Ray, after a tie, by Francis Ouimet. Walter Travis in particular owed his victory to his marvellous skill in the short game. He was a short driver and in the final at Sandwich he defeated Ted Blackwell, the world's "longest hitter," and it was all to the good of golf that skill and finesse should triumph over brute force.

With the enormously long courses in existence today, the big husky fellow has already too great an advantage, and there is no necessity for us to go out of our way to make things still easier for him.

Larger holes would also have the effect of eliminating the stymie in golf. The only man, in the long run, who suffers from the stymie is the player who cannot negotiate one.

We play golf for fun and to quicken our pulse rate, and so I do not see why we should be deprived of the joy of lofting a stymie and beating an opponent on the last green who apparently had our five dollars in his pocket.

It may be, and in fact often is, argued that stymies increase the element of luck in golf. I do not consider, however, that this is correct, but even if it were, is it so grave a disadvantage? As a matter of fact I believe that stymies increase the element of skill and not of luck.

In any case luck, or apparent luck, is the zest of life as well as golf, and I often think there is a great similitude between the problems of golf and everyday life.

It is a similar mind that, in the effort to eliminate the element of luck, would have the fairways and greens all dead flat. It is the undulations of the fairways—undulations like the swell of the Atlantic—which make some of the British seaside courses so exciting and interesting, and yet we have heard critics and professionals in particular condemn these courses because of their undulations. Indeed, only too often they have succeeded in persuading the natives to shave them down as money became available for them to do so.

The result is that in Britain, where they are spending money to destroy undulating features, golf courses are deteriorating, whereas in America, where they seem to be absorbing the true spirit of golf even to a greater extent than in its native home in Scotland, they are spending money to create the very features of undulating fairways which are being so ruthlessly destroyed in England. As a direct consequence, golf courses in America are becoming more enjoyable every year.

As an example, there is a public course at Bayside Long Island which we constructed recently. The land was most unsuitable for golf, as it was a flat farm intersected by stone walls. We pulled down the walls and made gently sloping undulations with the stones which we got in this way, and converted the whole of the rest of the ground, including the greens, into hollows and hillocks resembling the Scottish seaside courses, so that the whole area could be mown by machines.

We constructed only nineteen sand traps, and yet in spite of its natural disadvantages the course has become so interesting and popular that even in the days of the Depression they have obtained over ten thousand dollars each playing month in green fees—probably twice as much as any other recent golf club in New York State.

There are few things on a golf course more severely criticized than undulating greens, but players who have come to curse, remain to bless us at Bayside.

There was a golf course we made in Britain called Sitwell Park—which is illustrated in Robert Hunter's book on golf course architecture, *The Links*—where some of the greens were extremely undulating. Nevertheless, the course was so thrilling and popular that the club obtained eight hundred members.

A new committee was, in time, appointed who were influenced by the criticism of the unsuccessful professional competitors in an Open Championship, and they flattened out these undulating greens. The members lost their interest and many of them resigned, and today I understand that the membership is only one half of what it was originally.

Undulating greens are in reality easier than flat ones, as the undulations enable a good player to judge his distances, and moreover they provide excitement and thrills until the last putt is holed. Larger holes might give some temporary satisfaction owing to smaller scores, but in the long run would rob the game of a large part of its interest, excitement and thrill.

❧ *Financing Golf Courses* ❧

I was likening the element of luck in golf to luck in everyday life. Socialists who have already created destitution and misery for millions in Europe have a similar mentality to the anarchists of golf. They believe that success in life is due to luck and not to skill.

It would be well if the world could give more consideration to the words of Abraham Lincoln delivered to the Workers' Association in 1864.

> ❧ "Prosperity is the fruit of labour; prosperity is desirable, it is a positive good to the world. That one should be rich shows that others may become rich and hence is just encouragement to industry and enterprise. Let not he who is houseless pull down the house of another but rather let him work diligently and build one for himself, thus by example assuring that his own shall be safe from violence when built." ❧

We cannot have too many men of Abraham Lincoln's mentality using every endeavor to prevent the destruction of the old traditional spirit of the game which some of us hold so dear. Socialism is a real danger to golf and in fact every other game. A succession of governments with socialistic ideas, piling up increased taxes and rates on golf courses, have already retarded materially the growth of golf in Britain. Socialism is a policy of destruction and not construction. History has proved many times that it can only lead to misery and destitution.

Where capitalism is strongest the workers are richest, and where socialism is rampant the workers are destitute. How many golf courses are there in Russia? Under the capitalist system the luxuries of the rich, as in the case of motor cars in America, inevitably become the necessities of the poor.

It is only a question of time and steering clear of the fallacies of socialism for golf and golf courses to be available for all. There are far too many people who believe that you can benefit the poor by forcibly seizing the wealth of the rich. If wealth simply consisted of money, this might be possible, but money is only a medium for the exchange of wealth, and riches simply consist in factories, machinery and above all organization. You cannot steal organization, and factories and machinery are worthless without it.

I left Europe to reside in America because I felt that it was only a question of time for Europe to be destroyed by socialistic propaganda and legislation. It is with a feeling of alarm that I notice in the United States the spread of similar doctrines which has led to the misery of British workers.

In a time of temporary depression it is so easy to rouse the passions of the people and introduce legislation, like the British dole, which will simply accentuate and perpetuate the evils they are trying to cure.

There are an increasing number of Americans who honestly believe, notwithstanding the lessons of history, that wealth producing machinery creates unemployment and poverty. The present depression and unemployment is due entirely to a cessation in the production of wealth owing to the stock exchange crisis causing a stoppage in the use of wealth producing machines.

A wave of optimism succeeded by too great a wave of pessimism. It is the duty of every good golfer and citizen to dam this tide of pessimism and encourage counter propaganda to neutralize false economic doctrines, for if they do not do so, not only golf but everything else that is desirable will go.

There are many keen golfers who are millionaires and multimillionaires, and may I suggest that there are two ways in which they can expend their millions to bring health, happiness and prosperity to future millions. One is to give or leave their money to counteract the false economic doctrines which will inevitably destroy the prosperity of the world's workers, and the other is to spend or even lend their money for financing the initial capital expenditure of golf courses. In my experience the great difficulty in starting new golf courses is the initial capital expenditure on the land and the course.

When a club is formed there is no difficulty in making it a financial success and even paying off within a few years the capital that has been expended on it.

I would suggest, however, that no money be lent for constructing an elaborate club house. The first club of which I was a member had only a hundred dollar hut as a club house and beer and sandwich luncheons, yet we got as much health and happiness out of it as any other.

A hundred thousand dollars lent on the understanding that it would be repaid within a few years could be used over and over again for financing new golf courses, and would bring more health and happiness to the community than many times that amount expended in hospitals and other charitable ventures. Prevention is always better than cure, and nothing helps so much to keep people fit and well and out of hospitals than fresh air combined with exercise and pleasurable excitement.

❧ *Camouflage* ❧

I am sitting in my veranda at the present moment on the edge of the 6th fairway of the Pasatiempo Course. I have just remarked to my wife that there are two bunkers within a hundred yards of her capable of concealing a hundred soldiers in each and machine guns in a defensive position. One bunker not infrequently catches a sliced second shot at the sixth hole and the other a pulled tee shot at the seventh. She has seen them a thousand times and probably been in them fifty times, and I have asked her if she can show me their position from where we are sitting. She was quite unable to do so. "Imagine you are coming from the direction of an enemy attacking a fortified position. Would it be possible for you to get any idea where the defensive force was located?" and she admits it would not. As a matter of fact she hazarded a guess at the position of one of them, and although she had seen them literally hundreds of times before, when we went out to investigate we found that she was over twenty yards out in her reckoning.

The thought that was in my mind was that if every country made their defenses on similar lines it is obvious in land warfare an attacking force would always be wiped out and, if no one dare attack, war would cease. If all countries concealed their defensive positions this would be a far greater factor in preserving the peace of the world than all the efforts of the League of Nations or any other means.

Instead of the out-of-date slogan that "attack is the strongest form of defense," prove that the attacker will most certainly lose and there will be no more war.

A thoughtful golfer would immediately say, "But no well-designed and constructed golf course has concealed traps." This is true, but every bunker which has been constructed of a natural appearance, although extremely visible from the tee, is invisible when viewed from the opposite direction.

The secret of making a well-constructed golf course and a concealed fortification is in the imitation of Nature. It is clear that if a defensive position is indistinguishable from the natural objects or particularly the natural undulations of the landscape, it will escape the disagreeable attention of the enemy.

I have already stated that it was my observations of the

Boer War that first interested me in the imitation of Nature, what is now known as Camouflage.

I was fortunate during the war in being asked to give the demonstrations to the British Army Council which led to the establishment of the British School of Camouflage, and which was the forerunner of all the allied schools. Although the inception of the ideas which originated this school were suggested from observations of the methods of the Boers, yet the practical experience which enabled me to improve on them came from my experience as a golf course architect in the imitation of natural features.

There is a marked similarity in the mentality between the regular soldier and the professional golfer.

There was no subtlety in the old golf courses made by the professional golfer. Every hole was made on stereotyped lines with cross bunkers extending from the rough on one side to the rough on the other so as to prevent all outflanking movements. Similarly, the professional soldier makes all his defenses on a stereotyped pattern, trenches similar to the old golf course constructed in straight lines and angles and even topped with white sand bags so that the enemy can see them ten miles away.

On the other hand, the modern golf architect makes every golfing feature harmonize with nature so as to set a different strategic problem at every hole.

Similarly, the Camoufleur (expert on camouflage) makes every defensive position harmonize with the natural features of the landscape so that they will escape the observation of the enemy either from the ground or from the air.

❧ *Handicapping* ❧

I am convinced that the system of handicapping as adopted by the Royal and Ancient Golf Club of St. Andrews is the simplest and best. It does not require anyone to submit to the annoyance of taking out a card. The handicapping committee make your handicap according to your play against other members and not according to the course.

For example, they fix a handicap for Bobby Jones, Roger Wethered, or Cyril Tolley and then allot the handicaps of other players accordingly.

For instance, one of the committee will ask you how MacDonald is playing at present, and you reply, "Pretty well. I gave him three strokes and he beat me on the last green." The committee will then figure that as your handicap is nine they can safely give MacDonald eleven. If this system is simple and practical for St. Andrews, which has members scattered all over the world, it should be much easier for the average club.

It is only necessary for a golf club to fix the handicap of one of their best players relatively to that of Bobby Jones or some other crack player to get the handicap of every other member of the club. It may be objected that there are many clubs whose members have never played with Bobby Jones and not even seen him play. In this case there are certain to be some players who have played against members of other clubs who know what their handicaps are compared with the leading players.

Even if we were to take an extreme case, a club can always figure what their professional's handicap should be relative to an Open Champion, and the members can be handicapped from the professional. It is true that many professionals think they would lose caste if they were given handicaps, but I think this objection could be got over.

Many golfers will argue that handicapping against the par of courses has resulted in improvement of standardizing handicaps. This is quite true, but any rotten system is better than no system at all.

Previous to the attempt made to standardize handicaps, it was usual for a club to make their best player "scratch" and handicap from him. His real handicap might not be scratch at all but six or even ten. It should not be difficult for a club to fix the handicap of their best player and handicap their other members accordingly.

I cannot see how it is possible to fix the par of a golf course according to the length of the holes. I once lengthened a course over a thousand yards and the record was reduced by six strokes. The original course had small blind greens, and many of the fairways were on a pronounced hill slope bordered by long grass. When the course was lengthened, the greens enlarged and made visible, the long grass eliminated, and the hill climbing diminished, the record was reduced from seventy-four to sixty-eight.

Incidentally, as I have suggested before, it is no criterion of a good course that the record is high.

This is usually an indication of a bad course, and only too frequently means that the putting surfaces are untrue, the approaches unfair and the greens small and blind. On the contrary, if the average score is high but the records extremely low—sixty-four or sixty-five for a course under seven thousand yards—it usually means that a first class player gets full reward for accurate play.

As an alternative to handicapping from individuals, the system advocated by Max Behr has its advantages. He argues that as a player's value in match play is not based on his total score, but on his ability to play individual holes, his handicap should be based on these. He suggests that a man's handicap should be arrived at by deducting the number of holes he does in par from eighteen, with every hole he does in less than par counting an additional point. To take an example, supposing Bobby Jones does fourteen holes in par, two under and two over, then his handicap is scratch. If an inferior golfer does six holes in par and the remainder over then his handicap is eighteen minus six, or namely twelve. Handicaps over eighteen are given on equally simple lines. Max Behr's system eliminates the delay and irritation of finishing every hole, but even his system is based on the assumption that a course is always played from the same tees, whereas the system of handicapping from individuals as adopted at St. Andrews has none of these disadvantages.

I must admit that one of the reasons why I am prejudiced against handicapping from courses is that in time it must have the effect of standardizing them. The charm of golf is variety and there is no doubt that greater variety can be attained by changing the holes and tees from day to day.

It has been repeated *ad nauseam* in this book that golf is a game and not a mathematical business, and that it is of vital importance to avoid anything that tends to make the game simple and stereotyped. On the contrary, every endeavor should be made to increase its strategy, variety, mystery, charm and elusiveness so that we shall never get bored with it, but continue to pursue it with increasing zest, as many of the old stalwarts of St. Andrews do, for the remainder of our lives.

FINIS

❧ *Alister MacKenzie's Obituary* ❧

Dr. Alister MacKenzie, internationally famous golf course architect, author and founder of the Camouflage School, England, which all officers of the allied forces during the World War attended to learn camouflage, died early yesterday afternoon at his home at Pasatiempo. He was 63 years of age, a native of Scotland, and had resided in this city since March, 1930.

Funeral services will be held Tuesday at 11 o'clock a.m., with Rev. Norman H. Snow of the Episcopal church officiating: Inurnment will be in the Odd Fellows' mausoleum. Eventually the ashes will be sent to Dr. MacKenzie's old home in Scotland.

Dr. MacKenzie came back to the United States in 1927 especially to lay out the Cypress Point golf course. In 1929, he came to Santa Cruz and laid out the Pasatiempo course. He married Mrs. Edgar Haddock during that year and in 1930 built the home in which he died.

He had been ill only a short time and had been confined to his bed only two days. Surviving are the following: Mrs. MacKenzie, widow; two sisters, Miss Mabie MacKenzie and Dr. Marion MacKenzie; a stepson, G. Marston Haddock of San Francisco; Mrs. Haddock and two children.

Dr. MacKenzie had laid out and completed over 400 golf courses in England, Scotland, Australia, New Zealand and the United States, and was considered one of the best golf architects. He was consulting architect for the Royal and Ancient Golf Club of St. Andrews, Scotland. Among the principal courses in this country planned and laid out by him were Cypress Point, Pasatiempo and Augusta National. He also laid out the Buenos Aires Jockey Club park at Buenos Aires.

Dr. MacKenzie had just finished a book on golf, entitled "The Spirit of St. Andrews." This book has not yet been published. He was working on a book on camouflage at the time of his death. The introduction of "The Spirit of St. Andrews" was written by Bobby Jones, internationally famed golfer.

—*Santa Cruz Sentinel,* 1934